SUR
SECRETS
COLLEGE
STUDENTS

By
Mary Kay Shanley
and Julia Johnston

BARRON'S

All inquiries should be addressed to:
Barron's Educational Series, Inc.
250 Wireless Blvd.
Hauppauge, NY 11788
www.barronseduc.com

ISBN-13: 978-0-7641-3572-9
ISBN-10: 0-7641-3572-4

Illustrations by Tom Kerr

*Rankings on pages 44, 101, 116, 125, 175, and 206 courtesy of College Prowler, Inc.,
Campus411.com, and Academic Financial Solutions, LLC.*

Library of Congress Catalog No.: 2006102135

Library of Congress Cataloging-in-Publication Data
Shanley, Mary Kay, 1943–
    Survival secrets of college students / by Mary Kay Shanley and
Julia Johnston.
        p.   cm.
    Includes index.
    ISBN-13: 978-0-7641-3572-9
    ISBN-10: 0-7641-3572-4
    1. College student orientation.   2. College freshman—Life skills
guides. I. Johnston, Julia. II. Title.
LB2343.3.J64   2006
379.1'98—dc22   2006102135

Printed and bound in Canada
9 8 7 6 5 4 3 2 1

Contents

Introduction   vii

Chapter 1: That Long-Short Last Summer at Home   1
Curfews? You've Got to Be Kidding   1
Party, Party, Party   4
Seven Ways to Keep Your Parents Mostly Happy   5
Stuff You'll Worry About   6
Touching Base with the Roommate Stranger   9
The Thing About Leaving   12

Chapter 2: What to Take—or Not   14
Jeans, Sweats, Three T-Shirts—and a Tux?   14
More to College than Clothes   16
Computer Gear   22
Flip-flops and 13 Other Things You Can't Live Without   24
AP Physics Notes and 13 Other Things You'll Take but Never Need   25
Lugging Stuff from Home   26

Chapter 3: Orientation: You're New, You're Nervous, and
    You Need It   30
Organized Chaos   30
What Should You Get Out of Orientation?   34
People, People Everywhere!   35
Choosing Classes—Perils, Perks, and Luck   38
Registration   43
The Best Thing About Orientation   45
Parent Orientation (No Kidding!)   46

Chapter 4: Homesick Blues   49
Saying Good-bye: Tears, Fears, and Cheers   49
Missing Your Dog, Your Mother, Your Room, and Your Parents' Car   52
Homesickness—It's Real   55
Looking for Those New Best Friends   60
Facebook—Pervasive Procrastination Tool?   63
Oops, That Friendship Didn't Work Out   65

How to Spend an Entire Parents' Weekend with Your Parents   66
Going Home: Your Old Life Doesn't Fit the New You   69

Chapter 5: Roommates: Friends, Foes, or Somewhere in Between   73
First Person in the Room Gets the Best Bed—Sometimes   73
Movin' on In   76
Getting to Know You   79
Three's a Crowd? It Depends . . .   83
Rooming with Your High School Friend   84
  It's Awesome!   84
  It's Awful!   86
How *Not* to Drive Each Other Crazy   86
If Things Get Really Bad   91
Residence Assistants—All-Purpose Students   93
Sex and the Double Room   95

Chapter 6: An Rx for Roommate/Residence Hall Hassles   98
Who Comes in to Clean This Place?   98
Gross Showers, Who Left the Toilet Seat Up, and Who Peed
    on the Seat Again?   101
How Hard Can It Be to Do Laundry?   103
It's Like a Party 24/7   106
Where Is Everyone?   109
Minority Issues   110
Theft and Personal Safety   114

Chapter 7: Okay, Time to Study   117
Hey, This Isn't High School   117
Professors—Pretty Important People   124
Love/Hate 8 A.M. Classes   128
Best Study Tips   130
Best Study Hideouts   133
Testing, Testing   134
Learning to Love Deadlines—or at Least Pay Attention
    to Them   138
When Too Stressed = Depressed, Get Help   141

Chapter 8: Really? Free Time!   144
Activities and the Pursuit of Happiness   144
Enough Activities to Fill a Wall Calendar   146
"I'll Do It! I'll Do It!" Why Volunteering Is a Big Deal   148
That Thing About Overcommitment   151
A Wake-up Call for the Former High School Athlete   153
Intramural and Club Sports   156
Going Greek–No, Thanks   159
Going Greek–Definitely   161
Rush Week–Parties, Free Food, and Bonding   164
Balancing Job and School   168

Chapter 9: Stay Healthy: Good Food and Bad Colds   172
Food Courts, "Sneeze Bars," and Meal Plans   172
Where's the Best Free Food?   178
Twinkies and Junk Food–a Basic Food Group?   179
That Nasty "Freshman 15"   180
R.A.s Talk About Eating Disorders   183
Exercise Beyond Climbing One Flight of Stairs   185
I Was So Sick . . .   187
Staying Healthy Without Dr. Mom Around   189
When Chicken Soup Isn't Enough   191

Chapter 10: Love, Sex, Alcohol, and Drugs   193
You Really Still Love Your High School Sweetheart?   193
Hanging Out, Hooking Up, and (Sometimes) Dating   198
Frank Talk About Date Rape   202
So, Where's the Party?   203
Beer as Nutrition, Wine in a Box, Mixed Drinks in a Garbage Can   208
Drugs–Casual or Otherwise   214
Don't Drink? Don't Do Drugs? Where to Find Friends Like You   217

Chapter 11: Hey, Lend Me $20   221
Where Did All That Money Go?   221
Food, Glorious Food   224
Budget Smarts   225

Textbook$ 227
Living on Plastic   229
Hit by Hidden Costs   233
Really Cheap Fun   236

Chapter 12: Second Semester and Beyond   237
Back on Campus   237
Where to Get the Best Advice   239
Choosing a Major ... or Not   241
How-I-Found-My-Major Stories   245
Spring Break–Utopia or Myth?   247
Studying Abroad   251
Should You Transfer?   254

Chapter 13: Epilogue   258
Did Your Parents Get Smarter Since You Left Home?   258
Final Thoughts   260

Resources   262

Introduction

This is a book about how to get to and through your freshman year and beyond. It's a must-read because the tips, lists, information, insight, warnings, and stories come from current college students. They, more than anyone else, understand how you feel *right now,* including what you don't know, need to know, and want to know to make your soon-to-be life on campus a great experience.

Your college journey will be more scary, absorbing, challenging, and powerful than you can ever imagine. It is, quite frankly, life-changing. And for all you party animals out there, yes ... it will be a lot of fun. You can speculate with family and friends what it will be like, think about it until your head hurts, and dream for nights on end. But nothing may be as helpful as reading this book.

Your journey begins right after high school graduation, when you're positive you're finally an adult, only to discover that you are still a semi-youngster living in your parents' house. You continue through a myriad of experiences—actually getting something out of orientation, roommate highs and lows, residence hall life, whether to study or not, sex, alcohol, drugs, money, being sick, and whatever lies beyond first semester. At every turn, and maybe every day, you'll make decisions—whether to eat yourself into the Freshman 15, when to connect with professors, how to infuse quality into free time.

Parents have different reactions to all your freedom and decision making. There are "helicopter parents" who hover around and want to be involved in all decisions, and there are the other parents who are willing to let you take your lumps for everything but the Really Big Stuff, which makes sense. After all, you are responsible for yourself now. When you trip and fall (and you will), you're the one who will help yourself back up, as did the students in this book. For example, Alix talks about partying and hooking up too much first semester and deciding that wasn't who she wanted to be. James tells you about waking up in the E.R. with alcohol poisoning, how he got that drunk, and how he worked his way out of the mess. He wants you to know his story so you'll know what to expect.

So say all our students, most of whom were strangers to us in the beginning. We found them through networking, including asking strangers wearing college sweatshirts if they went to that college, and friends of friends on Facebook.com. They met us in coffee shops, and talked to us on their cell phones and via e-mail. We found individuals, each with his or her values. They are of different ethnicities, cultures, and economic means. They agreed to help you because they wished they'd had this book before *they* packed for college, and especially once they got there and the parents left them alone among a sea of unfamiliar faces. We are grateful to these students for sharing their tips for success as well as some of their most difficult feelings and experiences, hoping you'd benefit.

Students are identified by name, year, and school so you know these are real people talking about what's happening now, not 10 years ago. They speak as individuals, not as spokespeople for their schools. Additionally, they don't always agree with each other. Even if their advice were consistent, they cautioned that things might be different for you because you are your own person.

In addition, you'll find other important nuggets of key information you need, ranging from how cribbing from online research paper mills can get you into big trouble . . . to how you know it's time to break up with your long-distance sweetheart . . . to why young women should check with the family doctor or college health center about getting the vaccination against cervical cancer.

We thank the many people who helped make this book possible: our students; experts who responded to our many queries; friends, colleagues, and students not in the book who helped us find other students; Amy Rhodes, a terrific writer whose comments sharpened our chapters; and our husbands (we each have just one), who offered suggestions only when asked and listened to us whine about deadlines anytime. We are also grateful to our editor, Kathleen Ganteaume, whose guidance helped make this book worth your time to read.

We had fun writing this book, and we're sure you'll get a kick out of reading it, even packing it in your college bags for instant reference. We wish for you that you get all A's, friends who make you laugh, and special experiences to tell your friends back home. You may want to keep some of those experiences from your parents, though.

That Long-Short Last Summer at Home

What is with parents, anyway? They feel the need to impose curfews and rules when all you really want is to hang with friends. How are you ever going to make it through summer? Just do your best to accept the fact that it's a summer of polar-opposite emotions, sometimes within minutes. You want to be on campus and you're scared to leave home. You should be treated like an adult but you're still their child under their roof. You hang on to friendships, thinking all the while that good-byes are looming. But you'll try getting along with the parents (or at least coexisting), work more hours for college cash, and maybe e-mail that roommate stranger, a start to moving on. All the while, though, the only sure thing in your June–August world will be knowing that home and hometown will never be quite the same. So exciting. So bittersweet.

Curfews? You've Got to Be Kidding

Curfew definitely was an issue. I didn't think I had one, but my mom wanted me home about 12:30 (A.M.) and I had a habit of coming home between 1:30 and 2. I wasn't at bars but at some friend's house. It was part of wanting to get time together before we all left for college. Mom felt she had to get up when I came in, and I didn't think she did.

Diane Hennan, freshman, Saint Ambrose University, Davenport, IA

I'd argue with Mom that I would be living in DC soon, so why was she laying down the curfew laws? She told me I was living under her roof and needed to follow her rules. Looking back, it all makes sense. The day will come soon enough when you move out, so just soak up the last summer sun, as stressful as it is with the parentals.

Sarah Kiener, freshman, Catholic University of America, Washington, DC

GET THIS! YOU WANT TO LEAVE SO BADLY THAT . . .

- you've seen every movie and gone to the mall every day since May 14;
- you beg to go get boxes to start packing your stuff.

My parents were pretty strict and always nagging me to be on time, get in by curfew, have a decent bedtime. So first semester I took advantage of not being where my parents were and messed around a lot more than in high school. You get to be a lot more independent in college.

Jessica Monroe, sophomore, Butler University, Indianapolis

DID WE MENTION THAT . . .

Certain approaches to that prickly curfew issue tend *not* to work:

- Whining, as in "Nobody else has a curfew!"
- Playing the life's-not-fair card yet again.
- Lying, as in "Wow! We were playing poker and the time just got away from me!"
- Announcing that you are an adult now and can do what you want—even though you and your parents know you don't have enough money to live on your own for more than a week.

If your parents say the hurrah has to end at midnight, explain that "our age group likes to hang out after midnight, into the morning." Give them a decent argument, decently.

Scott Beggs, senior, Baylor University, Waco, TX

Everyone has one friend whose mom doesn't care when she comes home, and you can't compare everything she's allowed to do with what you should do.

Laura Polden, freshman, George Washington University, Washington, DC

Party, Party, Party

Don't do the teenage rebellion this summer because of your parents. You will have plenty of time to go to parties, be the rebel in college. They're just being protective.

Ben Petersen, freshman, Northern Arizona University, Flagstaff

---

Don't drive if you're drinking and don't do anything stupid with guys. We girls were really good about watching out for each other.

Anna Skelly, senior, California State University–Long Beach

My parents were pretty strict about curfew, so I found a way around it: I would come home on time, go to my room, and then climb out the window onto a chair in the backyard. I realized by the end of the summer they were on to me the whole time.

Anonymous

I didn't really party all summer because I had a 5 A.M. shift at the Y and had to teach children. So the last week before going to college I went on kind of a binge because I hadn't had time to say good-bye to people and it seemed the only way I could handle it. But I don't have happy memories from that; I'm completely fuzzy on it. Looking back, there were so many better things I could have done.

Alix Lifka-Reselman, freshman, Brandeis University, Waltham, MA

GET THIS! WHO ARE YOU?

> Sit down with yourself at the beginning of the summer and decide what kind of person you want to be. A smoker? Partyer? Good girl? Bad boy? Drinker? Nudist? Bible-thumping Christian? Shake yourself of the reputations and expectations from high school and your family. When you get to college, go about being that person.

Luke Roth, freshman, Loyola University, Chicago

You are supposed to be grown up, getting ready for college, being responsible. But that's the farthest thing from your mind. All you really want to do is hang out and do nothing.

Brittany Borstad, junior, Iowa State University, Ames

Seven Ways to Keep Your Parents Mostly Happy

1. It's finally hit Mom that you're leaving, even though it's not for good. Spend time with her each week or she'll start crying.

2. Share your mail/e-mail from the college so they'll know what's going on in your future life and won't feel like they're totally losing you.

3. Do the little things they want you to do, even stupid stuff like doing dishes, and maybe you'll get to stay out later, sometimes.

4. Go places with your parents. (We're not just talking restaurants.) You'll get points.

5. Stay over at a friend's house or go camping if you are going to do the alcohol or sex stuff rather than flaunt it in front of your parents.

6. Confession may be good for the soul but it's hardly ever good for the parents. There's a whole lot they wouldn't like to know about. Now or ever.
7. Work, work, and work to save money for college. And show them your growing bank account!

Stuff You'll Worry About

Whether I would make friends. Whether my roommate was going to be a weirdo. Whether I learned anything in high school.

Ian Young, sophomore, Grinnell (IA) College

That my friends and I would all go our separate ways and never have the same friendships we did when we graduated.

Jenn Mulroe, senior, University of Connecticut, Storrs

Will my roommate and I get along? Will she be gothic? Do we really have to wear shower shoes? If there's a fire drill while I'm in the shower, what will happen?

Shelly Haffner, sophomore, University of Wisconsin–Oshkosh

Going to a college if none of your friends will be there. I had a feeling that when I actually got there, I'd be in the same boat as everyone else.

Ross Kaplan, senior, Colby College, Waterville, ME

That I wouldn't bring the right stuff.

Lauren Press, junior, University of Denver

I was terrified at the thought of leaving for a place 12 hours away, where not a single face was familiar, and my boyfriend would be going to St. Olaf (MN).

Jackie Kohler, sophomore, Mercyhurst College, Erie, PA

Buying things. It seemed like all the stores were selling everything and I needed to get one of each color.

Sandra Lazo de la Vega, sophomore, Florida Atlantic University, Wilkes Honors College, Jupiter

That college would be like in the movies—going to class, going to parties. But it isn't much different than real life at home, and you end up feeling more comfortable than you thought you would.

Emily Cullings, junior, Colgate University, Hamilton, NY

Whether I would be able to cook some sort of meal, know how to clean up after myself, and pay rent. I left home the day after graduation for a job on the beach, and we had dishes everywhere. I called Mom and said, "I hate to ask you this, but how do you wash dishes?"

Austin Hudson, freshman, Mississippi State University, Starkville

My ability to keep up in college courses. I put a lot of pressure on myself to keep up the same level of achievement I had in high school. I found, though, that if I worked hard and talked to my professors about questions and concerns, I did well.

Claire K. Harris, junior, Vanderbilt University, Nashville, TN

Some (high school) teachers in trying to motivate us told us we'd never make it in college. But it wasn't as bad as I had thought it would be.

Jessica Monroe, sophomore, Butler University, Indianapolis

That spring I thought, "I can't do this." I'd never been away from home for more than two weeks. But I won a one-month trip to Germany for that summer with a group of students I didn't know, and this group of strangers all helped each other. I would not have made it through my freshman year without that experience. When I came home, I was confident and could make my own decisions. My parents had confidence in me and I fed off that and knew I could survive in college.

Bryn Rouse, sophomore, University of Montana, Missoula

GET THIS! HEY, NO PRESSURE

I didn't worry about much at all. That summer, I had less responsibility than I can ever remember. No summer reading, no summer courses or anything. I never felt any pressure about college because there wasn't much I could do to get ready when I didn't know what to expect.

David Neumann, sophomore, University of Southern California, Los Angeles

The only thing I worried about that really materialized was getting homesick. But going home for breaks and calling home helped.

Tyler Sloss, sophomore, Duke University, Durham, NC

Touching Base with the Roommate Stranger

I remember waiting to get that little green paper that had a name, address, and phone number of my roommate. She was from the rural South and I'm from a midwestern city. I called her and we did a few e-mails. And I Googled her.

Beth Giudicessi, senior, University of Notre Dame (IN)

We talked on the phone and e-mailed, trying to negotiate what to bring for the room. I brought a VCR-DVD player. We each brought our own mini-fridge because just one would be too small for four of us.

Olamide Oduyingbo, freshman, Quinnipiac University, Hamden, CT

She called me first. I'm a night-owl person and she gets up early to practice with the water polo team. So we talked about how we'd deal with that.

Antha Mack, freshman, University of California–San Diego

GET THIS! BEST REASONS TO E-MAIL THE ROOMMATE

- Instant feel for whom you'll live with for the next nine months
- Instant way to get parents off your back about contacting the roommate
- Instant dinner partner for that first night alone on campus

Don't say, "Hi, my name is blah-blah and I'm so excited about living with you!" If you seem too eager, you'll frighten them. On the other hand, if you seem apathetic, they'll think you don't want to room with them.

Sage Middleton, senior, Tulane University, New Orleans

I had two roommates. I talked to one of them for about 10 minutes on the phone (before school started). I never talked to the other one until we met.

Caitlin Wells, sophomore, Grinnell (IA) College

GET THIS! EXACTLY WHO *IS* MY ROOMMATE?

When I received my roommate assignment, it mentioned "Alexander." Although my parents and I were mildly concerned, we were all still quite excited that I was going away so far and thrilled about Brown. When I called her, a male voice was on the answering machine and I thought, "Okay, this is not just an error. I am going to be living with Alexander." Turns out it was an error, and Alexandra called me back promptly. She mentioned that she was going to bring hot pink sheets. I mentioned ecru, and she had no idea what that shade would be. She was extremely concerned that we match in our room. And thus started quite a disastrous freshman-year roommate relationship!

Sri Kalyanaraman, junior, Brown University, Providence, RI

Get a floor plan from the university so the two of you have an idea of what will fit where before you get to school.

Graham Shepherd, senior, DePauw University, Greencastle, IN

I didn't understand some things my roommate wrote or read until he told me he was dyslexic. I thought, "Already there's a wall down." He drove to Flagstaff from Alaska. When his truck broke down in Canada, he called and said, "Take extra-good notes at orientation and pick up my schedule and my books." Because we'd been e-mailing, we already sensed we'd get along.

Ben Petersen, freshman, Northern Arizona
University, Flagstaff

20/20 HINDSIGHT

My roommate and I were tentative on calling or e-mailing each other. It turned out we Googled each other and looked up profiles online. I felt like a stalker and didn't really learn anything. When I finally got up the guts to call her, it was a huge relief. I cleared up her fears of me being a small town Iowa hick with a mom named Bessie and a cow for a pet. And I learned that she wasn't a pretty princess pom girl who only wore pink.

Brenna Derksen, freshman, University of Iowa, Iowa City

The Thing About Leaving

It almost seemed like I was living every day just to leave town. I put so much focus on things I needed to do before moving that I forgot to take time to really enjoy my last summer at home. It didn't really hit me until I had been at school for a few months that I should have gone out more with my friends and taken more time with my family instead of rushing out the door.

Sarah Kiener, freshman, Catholic University of America, Washington, DC

I spent a lot of time with my friends because we were going to be scattering throughout the country. It's nice to have those memories to cherish. It was the last time we were all together.

Jennifer Herlihy, senior, University of California–Berkeley

GET THIS! WHO'S ON EDGE?

Every last one of you is
1. anxious about leaving home, figuring out campus, meeting new people;
2. nostalgic because home will never seem quite the same again;
3. scared. Just flat-out scared;
4. eager about the prospect of being in charge of you;
5. clueless about what "being in charge of you" actually means.

One of my favorite teachers had a great saying she told us as juniors: Seniors suddenly become mean because they want everybody to hate them so they don't have to say good-bye.

Alix Lifka-Reselman, freshman, Brandeis University, Waltham, MA

I was excited and nervous, but more nervous as school (and moving) got closer. Start preparing early, because as the summer comes to a close, the pressure of leaving grows quickly.

Amie Reed, junior, Illinois State University, Normal

Leaving home wasn't quite as bad for me because I went a year after my brother, so he got the brunt of smothering.

Ross Kaplan, senior, Colby College, Waterville, ME

GET THIS! SEVEN THINGS YOU'LL WANT TO DO BEFORE SAYING SAYONARA

1. Take a road trip with friends, even if it's only to the next county.
2. Go to lunch with a friend, and then drive around to other friends' houses, blasting songs you love.
3. Remind your parents there's still time to go shopping.
4. Send letters to friends you will miss. You'll write things you'd never say out loud.
5. Take little brothers and sisters somewhere you *all* want to go. Your parents might even send some money with you.
6. Give your parents a thank-you card with a movie certificate to use after you leave.
7. Burn a CD of your favorite songs and give a copy to each of your friends.

Chapter 2

What to Take—or Not

Okay, time to pack. All you have to do is decide what you'll need from your closet, your dresser drawers, desk, and the first 18 years of your life; fit all that into suitcases and duffel bags; and hope when you get to campus, there's enough space in your new postage-stamp-size room to unpack everything. It's such a huge project that moms often offer to help—or flat out take over. Take essentials, like posters or pictures that make the room your own space. And skip nonessentials, like school supplies that you can buy there. Whatever your choices, realize that the whole packing ritual can get emotional (for you and your mom) and regardless of planning, you will still over-pack.

Jeans, Sweats, Three T-Shirts—and a Tux?

No one tells you to pack loads upon loads of party clothes and elaborate costumes.

Allison McAndrew, sophomore, Williams College, Williamstown, MA

With the high school weekend social scene, you can get away with wearing T-shirts. Here, there's more of a need for a little tank top with some sparkle on it.

Raija Bushnell, freshman, DePauw University, Greencastle, IN

The way people dress is very different from high school. I knew it would be a little more formal because there's a business school (Wharton) and I saw a lot of students wearing suits. I had basic jeans and stick with that; I am in literature classes, not business.

Katharine McCormick, sophomore, University of Pennsylvania, Philadelphia

> Bring as many sweatpants and T-shirts as you can.
>
> *Abby Beaves, freshman, St. Cloud (MN) State University*

I brought so few clothes that at the end of the week, all of my laundry needed to be done. But I could do it in one load.

Lori Donovan, junior, St. Olaf College, Northfield, MN

Only bring clothes you will need for the season—dorm closets are so small. And when you move at the end of the year, you do not want to have a lot to pack up and carry out.

Lauren Krpan, sophomore, University of Mississippi, Oxford

Are you in denial of the climate where you will be going to school? I brought a lot of summer stuff to New England and wore it twice.

Katia Porzecanski , sophomore, Tufts University, Medford, MA

Freshman year, I made fun of my roommate's heavy boots and ugly coat. Then a blizzard hit right before Christmas break and I had to walk through three feet of snow in sneakers. For Christmas that year, I bought boots and an even uglier coat than my roommate's.

Anonymous

Cheap sandals are definitely the way to go—you can roll out of bed, put a good pair of waterproof sandals on, and have that be your shoes for the day, including the shower. And a pair of standard black ones for everything else.

Luke Roth, freshman, Loyola University, Chicago

20/20 HINDSIGHT

Even though my mom supervised and my brother had already been to college, I brought too many clothes. But that's better than not enough, because you're already nervous about everything else. Clothes aren't something you should have to worry about.

Ross Kaplan, senior, Colby College, Waterville, ME

More to College than Clothes

Space in your room will be an issue more than anything else.

Austin Hudson, freshman, Mississippi State University, Starkville

No matter what, you will bring way too much stuff.

Chelsea Chaney, junior, Washburn University, Topeka, KS

Contact the people who lived in your room last year, which is easy with an advanced search on Facebook.com. I e-mailed them questions about room size.

Christina Hoffman, junior, Harvard University, Cambridge, MA

You buy way too much. There's a huge market to tell freshmen they need all this stuff, like extra-long sheets.

Jennifer Herlihy, senior, University of California–Berkeley

I brought literally everything to college. Probably because I have a younger brother and sister at home and I didn't want them to have my stuff.

Adrienne May, sophomore, University of Missouri–Kansas City

DID WE MENTION THAT . . .

We know a student who finally found the college's what-you-need list underneath the last pile of whatever he was cramming into a box a couple of hours before it was time to leave home.

GET THIS! YOUR GREAT-GRANDFATHER'S GOLD WATCH

> Don't bring anything you absolutely do not want to lose. People borrow. Things get lost, sometimes stolen.

Eighty percent of what I bought, I didn't need. Like a medium fridge I used about twice. It was a pain in the butt to move around and it took up a lot of room.

Sandra Lazo de la Vega, sophomore, Florida Atlantic University, Wilkes Honors College, Jupiter

GET THIS! THE SHOULD-I-BRING-IT TEST

> Key questions to ask yourself:
> - What items do I use during a typical day and night?
> - Look at every one of those things and consider: "If I don't have this at college, will I die?"
> - What about multiples—six pairs of pajamas, five toothbrushes, four sets of sheets? How long do I plan to be a college student, anyway?
> - Is there stuff I'll need once a week or once a semester? Once a week—bring it. Once a semester—borrow it.
> - Do I really need more than one towel?
> - Do I have to water it? Feed it? Trim it? Clean it? Leave it for the parents.
> - Do I get to eat it? Bring it.
> - How much stuff can I cram into plastic crates from Target?
> - Where will I store everything during the summer?

My parents hadn't gone to college in the United States and I hadn't lived in the United States for long, so I didn't know exactly of what items a typical dorm room consisted. I'm very used to a simple, Bohemian sort of lifestyle, but most students at Brown weren't. People basically packed up their whole room at home in a car and brought it with them!

Sri Kalyanaraman, junior, Brown University, Providence, RI

I cannot stress enough to bring posters, pictures, decorations, whatever you need to make your room a place you will enjoy. You'll spend a *huge* chunk of time there. I did not really decorate my side of the room, whereas one of my suitemates covered his entire wall with movie posters. We spent more time hanging out in his room than in mine.

David Neumann, sophomore, University of Southern California, Los Angeles

I've actually used everything I brought. People borrow my duct tape and Band-Aids. I live in a suite with five other girls and we like to cook one night a week, so we've used the plates and silverware.

Katie Beno, freshman, Gonzaga University, Spokane, WA

I brought an iron and ironing board because I like to have my clothes creased and pressed. People ask me to iron a shirt for them if they're going out at night.

Cassius Harris, sophomore, Oberlin (OH) College

I bought a lamp at Target and some envelopes, paper, pens, and I splurged on a TV. I'm a minimalist so I got along totally fine until Thanksgiving. Some freshmen show up with U-Hauls.

Lori Donovan, junior, St. Olaf College, Northfield, MN

DID WE MENTION THAT . . .

We hear that a TV is a disaster—nice for movie nights, but it's so distracting, you'll spend the majority of your free time in front of it, in which case you might not score so well on that math test, but you'll know what's happening on all your favorite soaps. Yeah, you'll actually start watching soaps.

I brought a life-sized baby palm tree, string lights, tank tops, and flip-flops from Phoenix to South Bend—even though in only a few weeks the weather would turn into an eternal blizzard. She brought sweatshirts. She hates my palm tree and I despise the agonizing, unbearable, yearlong Midwestern winters. Even so, we are great friends.

Nikki Hasbun, freshman, University of Notre Dame (IN)

DID WE MENTION THAT . . .

This student we know just had to take all her art gear, including a portable easel, huge drawing pad, and art books—even though she wasn't going to major in art or take an art class freshman year. In May she trucked art gear, dust and all, 1,500 miles back home. As she said, if it's not your focus, you'll never do it.

Get earplugs. My roommate had to wake up at 6:30 for class.
I didn't have class till 10. She tried to be quiet. And I wore earplugs.
You can't hear anything with earplugs, like radio or TV or even
humming.

Rosie Gregg, sophomore, Baylor University, Waco, TX

Take really good bedding. I brought my little security blanket, too.
It's soft and has my name on it in purple letters.

Meghan Hannahs, junior, Westminster College, Salt Lake City

If appliances aren't supplied in your dorm pod, bring a microwave for
tea and popcorn. A microwave is more versatile than a little coffeepot.
And a mini-fridge for lunches and milk.

Bryn Rouse, sophomore, University of Montana, Missoula

If you come a long way from home, bring the bare minimum and
buy what you need when you get here, like picture frames, nail
polish, and a stapler.

Laura Polden, freshman, George Washington University, Washington, DC

If you wait to buy things until you get to school, that's okay. But
here, everything will say "Tufts University" on it.

Katia Porzecanski, sophomore, Tufts University, Medford, MA

Computer Gear

I brought a desktop computer and a laptop.
I play computer games, so I need more power
than a laptop has.

Antha Mack, freshman, University of California–San Diego

I only have a laptop and it's better that way.
You can't bring a desktop to the library or
someone else's room, or take it home on break.

Emily Cullings, junior, Colgate University, Hamilton, NY

> Get a laptop. If
> your computer
> is large and
> unwieldy, you
> will regret it.
> You'll use a lap-
> top for almost
> everything.
>
> *Nathan Pflueger,
> freshman, Stanford
> (CA) University*

I would take my laptop to class, but it was distracting because I'd IM
friends and check the *New York Times*. I eventually decided to take notes
conventionally with a notebook and pen, although I'd bring my Mac
and occasionally send IMs.

Jennifer Herlihy, senior, University of California–Berkeley

20/20 HINDSIGHT

My very first week here, I had to take my laptop into the shop
and get brand-new MS Office and other software. It cost close
to $500. There was probably a list somewhere for what you
need, but I didn't know that the version on my computer
wouldn't work here. It's important to have everything up to
date. I was without my computer for the first two weeks.

Tanner Kokemuller, freshman, Colorado State University, Fort Collins

DID WE MENTION THAT . . .

▶ One student notes that about one-fourth of the students in his chem lab brought laptops to class, and 75 percent of them were paying more attention to whatever was on their laptop than to what the professor was saying. Regardless, our student suggests that if you actually want to focus and can type faster than you can write, a laptop is good.

You already are paying fees for computer use. You have computers to use in the dorm, in labs, and in the library seven days a week. Why would I take my small desk space in my room when a computer is available during the day? The Internet is free; you can e-mail, surf, and do spreadsheets.

Bryn Rouse, sophomore, University of Montana, Missoula

You don't *need* a printer, but it's very nice when you are doing a paper and you don't have to walk across campus at midnight in the cold to the library or lab to print out.

Diane Hennan, freshman, Saint Ambrose University, Davenport, IA

You want a printer and copier so you can copy somebody's notes.

Katie Beno, freshman, Gonzaga University, Spokane, WA

USB drives are really handy for storage. They allow easy transport of papers and projects, and they also are a good source of backup.

Amie Reed, junior, Illinois State University, Normal

GET THIS! PACKING CHECKLIST FOR YOUR COMPUTER

▶ Don't forget

- a power adapter;
- a surge protector;
- correct cables, most likely an Ethernet (CAT5) cable for the Internet and a USB cable for the printer;
- extension cords;
- 3-prong to 2-prong adapters, if you'll be living in an older dorm;
- original CDs for programs like Windows in case you have to reinstall something;
- a lock for your laptop computer, even in your room;
- extra ink cartridges. If you get those expensive extra cartridges before leaving home, guess who pays for them.

Flip-flops and 13 Other Things You Can't Live Without

1. Alarm clock number one because your parents aren't going to tiptoe into your room, tap you on the shoulder, lean down, and whisper, "It's time to get up. Class starts in half an hour. I turned on your shower and put a glass of juice on your desk. Have a good day."

2. Alarm clock number two because some mornings, one just isn't enough. Make sure this one doesn't have a snooze button.

3. A desk lamp because your room will probably have only one dim light and your roommate might actually go to bed early.

4. Extension cords with multi-outlet things.

5. A sewing kit and patches. (One student we know used a washcloth to patch a hole in her pants. Creative. Different, but creative.)

6. Microwaveable GladWare (containers) to store food you bring back from the dining hall or food your parents send. The small size is perfect for microwaving one package of ramen noodles or a can of soup.

7. A clothes hamper that's stretchy and holds *a lot*, because guess who's in charge of laundry now!

8. Hangers. You'll need them right away.

9. Duct tape for almost everything: it sticks your posters to the walls, gets rid of those little carpet fur balls the vacuum can't suck up, and works as a lint roller.

10. An umbrella or any other bad-weather gear. You'll regret not having it the first day you have to walk to class in the rain.

11. Floor pillows. Throw them under the bed when you don't need them.

12. Heavy-duty trash bags to carry things back and forth from home.

13. Butterfly chairs you can just fold up and put away when everybody finally leaves your room.

AP Physics Notes and 13 Other Things You'll Take but Never Need

1. A plasma TV. The screen is so big you'd have to stand out in the hall to watch it.

2. Twenty pairs of shoes. Fifteen or 16 pairs will go back home at Christmas.

3. Plastic washable dishes. They're a hassle to store and clean up, and paper plates are cheap and work just as well.

4. Your high school yearbook. Even if it is digital with videos and music and a ton of photos. Almost always, you keep high school friends and make college friends and never the twain shall meet.

5. Almost all of your graduation presents. Nobody needs three laundry bags and 16 picture frames.

6. Board games like Monopoly and Life. When was the last time you played Monopoly, anyway?

7. That guitar you expect to sell because you never had time to learn to play it.

8. A trash can. Your college already has them, although they might not match your bedspread.

9. A car. If you live and work on campus, you'll walk everywhere anyway.

10. The little dust-collecting figurine Grandma gave you.

11. Metal cups. They explode in a microwave.

12. Your hermit crab—although it is nice to have something to take care of besides yourself.

13. Your favorite books, unless you plan to read them between the hours of 3 and 9 A.M.

Lugging Stuff from Home

Pack light.

Andrew Lack, senior, Iowa State University, Ames

I realized I took way too much and was flying home at Christmas break with my bonsai tree.

Sarah Sentz, sophomore, University of Montana, Missoula

GET THIS! THE JURY'S STILL OUT ON PHOTO ALBUMS

I made a photo album from tons of pictures I took of everything I loved about my home, favorite restaurant, friends, family, work, and places I loved to visit. Some nights I go through the album and call everybody to see how they are.

Ben Petersen, freshman, Northern Arizona University, Flagstaff

I brought 15 photo albums my first two years, but not this year. Last summer, I got a digital camera, scanned all the photos I really love, and put them on my laptop. You can make a compilation of photos for people's Christmas presents.

Meghan Hannahs, junior, Westminster College, Salt Lake City

Put stuff you'll need right away in the same boxes or duffel bags. Pack things together that aren't essential and unpack them later. Have a travel kit with all the travel-size stuff you need the first two nights.

Kelly Schroeder, junior, University of Kansas, Lawrence

We borrowed a roof carrier and I ended up with two suitcases and four garbage bags full. It was good until the bags melted on my clothes.

Alix Lifka-Reselman, freshman, Brandeis University, Waltham, MA

Over the years, the packing thing has gone down. Now we fit everything in a Subaru instead of a Ford 350 pickup.

Meghan Hannahs, junior, Westminster College, Salt Lake City

For a girl moving out to Washington DC, I could not wait to get the heck out of my little city! No lie—all my things were packed and ready to go by the middle of June.

Sarah Kiener, freshman, Catholic University of America, Washington, DC

I packed two suitcases, max 50 pounds each, to fly to school. It was quite a challenge!!!! My room was definitely the "hermit" room because I had so few items there.

Sri Kalyanaraman, junior, Brown University, Providence, RI

GET THIS! WHICH PACKER ARE YOU?

1. The Procrastinator: Three hours before you go, throw it all into suitcases, duffel bags, boxes, crates, cubes, or just the back of the car. Save room for your parents to go with you.

2. The Backpacker: Roll up almost everything except sport coats, squeeze it into a huge duffel bag. What doesn't fit, you surely don't need.

3. The Parent: For the wrinkle-obsessed, fold flat with few creases and in tissue, lay everything in the bottom of the suitcase, and don't put your shoes on top.

4. The Grabber: Grab everything on hangers and drape it over whatever is already in the trunk.

FYI, by sophomore year, you'll use the shoving-the-elephant-into-the-duffel-bag approach and show up at school with all your stuff, but not really know how you pulled it off.

GET THIS! SCENT OVERLOAD

Avoid cologne or perfume all over your clothes by placing it (or any other liquids) in a plastic bag that seals closed. If flying, check the Transportation Security Administration site www.tsa.gov for the latest rules for liquids, gels, and other items allowed in carry-on and checked luggage.

I took a plane to school, but since I hate flying, I didn't check baggage. So I just showed up with a backpack. My roommate was driving to school, so I shipped her a box of clothes. Actually, though, I don't suggest just taking a backpack.

Lori Donovan, junior, St. Olaf College, Northfield, MN

20/20 HINDSIGHT

Get packed as soon as possible because that reduces a lot of stress. I didn't do it but I can look back and see if I had done that, we wouldn't have had a fight about it.

Diane Hennan, freshman, Saint Ambrose University, Davenport, IA

GET THIS! THE PARENT PSYCHE— IT'S REAL!

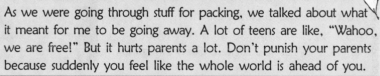

As we were going through stuff for packing, we talked about what it meant for me to be going away. A lot of teens are like, "Wahoo, we are free!" But it hurts parents a lot. Don't punish your parents because suddenly you feel like the whole world is ahead of you.

Alix Lifka-Reselman, freshman, Brandeis University, Waltham, MA

Chapter 3

Orientation: You're New, You're Nervous, and You Need It

Orientation starts with a wham-bang, whirlwind, day-night introduction to college life that you'll remember the rest of your life. Some say it's the best thing since popcorn, providing a preview of the new and different life to come, as well as helping anxious (and sometimes awkward) freshmen connect with one another. Others say besides learning the campus layout and surviving registration, orientation's a waste of time. Whatever. You still have to create your class schedule and register. Neither is easy or ever perfect, and both take you one giant step forward in the maturation process. When you're finished, you should be a bit wiser.

Organized Chaos

Do orientation. You won't regret it.

Katie Jozwik, junior, Columbia College, Chicago

I loved orientation. Everything is new, everyone is really happy, and the school is making a special effort to get you excited. Even though it

> Orientation introduces you to how much things will change.
>
> *Rachel Pfennig, freshman, DePauw University, Greencastle, IN*

can be a little daunting, try to be out and about socializing, because once classes start, people will get into their routines and it becomes a lot harder to meet people or to explore new things.

Gina Turrini, junior, Amherst (MA) College

Orientation was two days of hell, in the summer, weeks before school started. Staying in the dorm for one night is not anywhere near the same as staying in the dorm during the school year. It was mostly just informational stuff that I didn't want to know. The most beneficial was learning the layout of the campus, getting my ID card, and choosing my schedule.

Amie Reed, junior, Illinois State University, Normal

They housed you with people who would be in your dorm, so you had instant friends. But I blew off a lot of the advice they gave that doesn't apply to everyone. For example, don't work your first semester, but if you have done it in high school, it can work.

Jennifer Herlihy, senior, University of California–Berkeley

I thought orientation would be structured, like being in high school again. "Be here at 8:30." "Do this." "Do that." But orientation makes you aware of all the school's services. Even if you don't realize at the time that orientation is good for you, you'll figure it out later.

Henna Messina, senior, Fordham University, New York

You'll get a sinking feeling no one is telling you anything useful. That feeling is right.

Luke Roth, freshman, Loyola University, Chicago

GET THIS! THREE THINGS *NOT* TO DO AT ORIENTATION

1. Announce to your orientation group, "This would be so fun to do with my parents."
2. Hook up with someone in your group the first night. You have to spend a lot of time together, so it's best not to make it as awkward as possible.
3. Take orientation too seriously. Part useful, part fun, part boring, and over in a few days.

We divided into eight-person groups with a leader like back at camp, so we joked about "Camp Brandeis." Groups did different events like eating together and going to a carnival. At the same time we had mixers and shared stories at our hall meetings. Then all of a sudden I realized I had friends.

Zack Barr, freshman, Brandeis University, Waltham, MA

Sophomores lead you through what is essentially summer camp on steroids. You're out in the middle of the night running through fountains. You're so exhausted when school starts, you're not able to be homesick.

Beth Giudicessi, senior, University of Notre Dame (IN)

When I was a freshman at another college, we had a hoedown dance or whatever dumb thing. It was intimidating. You'd meet a new person every 30 seconds and the next day, you didn't know their names.

Brittany Borstad, junior, Iowa State University, Ames

An adviser told me to sign up for more (activities) than I thought I could handle because I'd realize I liked one thing better than another.

Jason Kaplan, senior, Colgate University, Hamilton, NY

Orientation is really a few days for you to deal with and resolve all these new things that have come into your life and the old things that will not be there anymore.

Sri Kalyanaraman, junior, Brown University, Providence, RI

DID WE MENTION THAT . . .

Skip your shower, skip your campus tour, but don't skip the activity fair.

20/20 HINDSIGHT

An intensive application process ensures that only the peppiest, friendliest, most welcoming upperclassmen are orientation group leaders. I thought it was silly that they would run us ragged for four days. But now I realize that keeping students busy is a good way to keep them from getting homesick, and it was a good introduction to college life.

Michael Salvati, junior, Villanova University, Philadelphia

My student leader was a little too excited. It freaked me out because she was always wanting me to go to everything. They had sporadic, 30-minute events so you didn't get to know anyone because you had to move on.

Sandra Lazo de la Vega, sophomore, Florida Atlantic University, Wilkes Honors College, Jupiter

It was the most overwhelming experience I've ever had. It was the end of June, early July, and so hot it was disgusting. You want to look so cute for all the potential boys. And I was just sweaty.

Laura Polden, freshman, George Washington University, Washington, DC

There's a fine line between perkiness and being really annoying during orientation. I admit I got a lot more out of orientation than I thought I would, but when it's 8 in the morning on day four of Freshman Orientation and your counselor's shrieking the lyrics to the school fight song, it can be a little much.

Anonymous

What Should You Get Out of Orientation?

Orientation has done its job if you

1. make at least one new friend;
2. can navigate campus, locating great spots to hang out, relax, eat, and study;
3. put on your first school T-shirt and begin to feel school pride;

4. figure out which services will be most helpful. After all, you've already paid for most of them. (Okay, your parents paid for most of them.);

5. decide the time is *now* for creating new experiences.

So says *Elizabeth Higgins, coordinator of Orientation & Judicial Affairs, University of Idaho, Moscow.*

People, People Everywhere!

You are going places and meeting people constantly, don't remember any names, but it's still kind of a cool thing. I was really nervous, but once you start seeing people, everyone is nice, you're having a good time, and it seems like college is going to be okay.

Ian Young, sophomore, Grinnell (IA) College

What I did *not* get was very much sleep—we stayed up talking until the wee morning hours just about every night. I met some of my best friends in the world.

Ryan Scofield, senior, College of William and Mary, Williamsburg, VA

I hit it off with this girl and after a couple of days, she asked if I would mind putting in a request to be her roommate. It worked out fine.

Cristina Baptista, graduate student, Fordham University, Bronx, NY

DID WE MENTION THAT . . .

If you really click with someone in orientation, try signing up for the same class. At the least, that can make the class more fun.

I met another guy and we hung out and at the end, decided to room together. Almost everyone else had to wait for a letter from Drake about their future roommate.

Justin Brookens, freshman, Drake University, Des Moines, IA

20/20 HINDSIGHT

Keep an open mind. I thought the South was backwards and had a lot of rednecks, but as soon as I got down here, my opinions changed because everyone is so hospitable and charming!! You have to look at things through other people's eyes to get a real impression of a place.

Lauren Krpan, sophomore, University of Mississippi, Oxford

Keep in mind that your best buddy at orientation may be the most irritating person on campus come September.

Anonymous

Orientation is a very long, isolated day if you aren't with a friend. That makes it scary. Try to make a friend early in the day—even if that person is only a friend for that day.

Anna Skelly, senior, California State University–Long Beach

I was a little nervous, going from a town of 1,200 to a big university (11,000+). It helped that my friend was with me.

Lisa Moody, freshman, University of Nebraska–Omaha

GET THIS! FITTING IN

Leave your pride at home. Come to college understanding that you are not the big fish in the small pond anymore.

Colleen Johnson, freshman, Webster University, St. Louis, MO

Awkwardness is a big thing in college. If you are able to accept that many (if not most) situations in college will be awkward, then you're one step toward getting on with your life without fretting about what people think about you.

Allison McAndrew, sophomore, Williams College, Williamstown, MA

The first person you recognize from high school, you freak out and want to latch onto, even if you never spoke to that person before. It's like finding the U.S. Embassy in a foreign country. But try not to do this, because orientation is your number one opportunity to meet as many people as you can.

Brittany Borstad, junior, Iowa State University, Ames

I kept thinking, "Why am I here with all these people I don't know when I could be with my friends who were still home?" That's short-term thinking. Be on campus, meeting your new friends.

Chelsea Chaney, junior, Washburn University, Topeka, KS

> ## GET THIS! ORIENTATION-SPEAK
>
> Everyone asks these questions:
> 1. What's your name?
> 2. Where are you from?
> 3. Which dorm do you live in?
> 4. What's your major?

I'm shy, quiet around people I don't know. But suddenly, because of orientation, you know several new people. You don't really realize how it happens, but it is nice.

Meghan Hannahs, junior, Westminster College, Salt Lake City

You meet a lot of kids. Later, you'll be walking down the road and someone will say, "Hey, I was in your orientation group." It really expands your lifelines at school.

Harrison Macris, sophomore, Boston University

Choosing Classes—Perils, Perks, and Luck

When I received the course catalog, I circled all the courses I was interested in taking. Of course, there were way too many.

Jason Chen, junior, Vassar College, Poughkeepsie, NY

Go to the earliest orientation session you can. I went to the first of 10 sessions at USC, which meant I had my pick of classes.

David Neumann, sophomore, University of Southern California, Los Angeles

Take the minimum load of 12 hours first semester. You'll be playing it by ear as far as what's required of your time because you still have to learn how much time is available.

Tiffany Wood, junior, Westminster College, Salt Lake City

20/20 **HINDSIGHT**

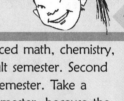

First semester I took 17 units, including advanced math, chemistry, and psychology. I've never had such a difficult semester. Second semester I took 13 units and had my easiest semester. Take a tougher fall semester and lighten up spring semester, because the days are nice, and you don't feel as refreshed after Christmas. And easier classes don't assign work during spring break.

Maria Henning, junior, University of California–Berkeley

Get your hardest classes out of the way first. You've just come out of high school so you are more focused, and still have a steady study schedule.

Elizabeth Pitruzzello, senior, Central Connecticut State University, New Britain

I was just taking general classes and had little say about them for my first semester. It's nice not to have to worry about choices freshman year. Classes got more complicated after that because I wanted more choices about times and days and you've heard about professors' reputations.

Beth Giudicessi, senior, University of Notre Dame (IN)

Take classes that make you think outside the box—music, theater, dance. Classes for your major are time-consuming, so this goofing off is good.

Annon Woodin, senior, Iowa State University, Ames

First semester I took all afternoon classes and realized I was wasting time. Second semester I ended up with morning classes. You get done by noon and have time to do more things. Plus, you rediscover naps.

Niki Grangruth, senior, St. Olaf College, Northfield, MN

Freshman year is your chance to really experiment, because you'll have the chance to take one or two electives. If you see that "conversational welding" class, and it looks like something you'd really like, take it!

Nick Hunter, senior, Massachusetts Institute of Technology, Cambridge

The professors chose movies to show one night of orientation. I chose movies that pertained to my interest and professors I wanted to get to know. You'd sit on couches and talk afterward. I made connections I've preserved.

Sandra Lazo de la Vega, sophomore, Florida Atlantic University, Wilkes Honors College, Jupiter

DID WE MENTION THAT . . .

You don't have to be a genius to CLEP (College-Level Examination Program) out of classes and still get class credit. That might not make your wallet fatter, but it's still money saved. Check online for tests offered at your school. Or call the school's testing center for deadlines.

The CLEP tests were so much easier than actual classes. It saved my parents money, and for me, time and my GPA.

Colleen Thurston, junior, University of Arizona, Tucson

Upperclassmen helped us choose classes to fulfill requirements. They didn't say, "This is a good professor, or not" because there are so many professors for your standard math and English classes. You'll get that kind of help from upperclassmen later in the year, as you begin to figure out what's going on.

Harrison Macris, sophomore, Boston University

I didn't plan that well, exploring things that were interesting, and ended up taking some courses that weren't required. Planning is tough as a (first-semester) freshman because you just got to school and don't know what's going on.

Lauren Press, junior, University of Denver

GET THIS! SECRETS TO A NEARLY PERFECT SCHEDULE

- You can't be in two places at once. Make a rough draft of your schedule to see where everything falls.
- Keep your classes together, if possible. Otherwise, you sit down to study and have to get back up and go to class.
- Don't underload on your classes. Dropping one later is easier than adding.
- You can drop a hellish class without penalty—*if you complete the paperwork by the drop date.*
- One-hundred-level classes are introductory; 200-level have more depth; 300-level are for seniors. The higher the number, the more work.
- It may take some serious caffeine to make it through some introductory courses, so get them over with freshman year.
- If you sort of, kind of, know what majors you're interested in, get a list of the classes you will need.

Most people take Pass/Fail for classes they know will be difficult but that they're interested in. If all you want to do is get out of the class with a passing grade, the P/F option is one way to go.

Caitlin Wells, sophomore, Grinnell (IA) College

GET THIS! BRYN'S BRILLIANT ADVICE ABOUT 200- AND 300-LEVEL CLASSES:

- Don't jump there freshman year because you don't fully understand how to study and manage your time.
- If you haven't taken AP classes in high school, you have to learn how to write essays, do more homework, and get note-taking skills.
- You'll be more on your own to understand the lecture and take notes.

Bryn Rouse, sophomore, University of Montana, Missoula

Registration

Before registration, make absolutely sure your financial aid is in impeccable order. Go over everything twice.

Henna Messina, senior, Fordham University, New York

Be flexible because your schedule won't be like you want. I got all my second options for classes.

Sarah Sentz, sophomore, University of Montana, Missoula

> ### GET THIS! WHEN THE CLASS YOU DESPERATELY WANT IS CLOSED
>
> - E-mail the professor and ask if there is room.
> - Schools, like airlines, overenroll classes, because the first week, kids end up dropping. Go to the first class and ask to get in.
> - Check online periodically to see if anybody has dropped.
> - Ask the department faculty to pull strings. (If you visit the office frequently, they get to know you and may be willing to be an advocate.)
> - Claiming that the 8 A.M. time you are scheduled for interrupts your sleep will not get you into the 11 A.M. class.

At my school, registration depends on how many credits you already have. So the older you are, the earlier you get to choose classes. If there is a class you really want, have an upperclassman enroll in it and then drop it when you are enrolling, so one spot opens up and you get it. To synchronize the drop and enroll, sit next to each other at computers. You should have the class number typed in. Then, right when the upperclassman drops the class, you press "enroll."

Kelly Schroeder, junior, University of Kansas, Lawrence

I'd heard horror stories about how freshmen can't get into anything. I had enough high school credits from AP and I.B. (International Baccalaureate) that I was able to register before most other freshmen. It's nice to have *x* number of credits to graduate early, but even nicer when it comes to registering for classes.

Sandra Lazo de la Vega, sophomore, Florida Atlantic University, Wilkes Honors College, Jupiter

---

GET THIS! TOP 10 BEST FACILITIES

1. University of Oregon, Eugene, OR
2. Vanderbilt University, Nashville, TN
3. University of Delaware, Newark, DE
4. Texas A&M University, College Station, TX
5. University of Arizona, Tucson, AZ
6. Amherst College, Amherst, MA
7. University of Central Florida, Orlando, FL
8. University of Florida, Gainesville, FL
9. Arizona State University, Tempe, AZ
10. Marquette University, Milwaukee, WI

The Best Thing About Orientation

Getting a feel for being on campus on your own and not with your parents. I hardly saw my dad. And staying up to 3 A.M. talking to people, taking a group night walk to the monuments, going to casino night. And then you have to go home for the rest of the summer.

Laura Polden, freshman, George Washington University, Washington, DC

Learning the building locations. It is so stressful to show up at college with no idea how to get to a class that is three-quarters of a mile away from your dorm.

Jenn Mulroe, senior, University of Connecticut, Storrs

GET THIS! STUFF YOU'LL ALSO HEAR ABOUT ...

- The writing center. Someone really good at English reads your papers and gives you feedback. A friend will say your paper's good so as not to hurt your feelings.
- A hotline. Ask pretty much any question.
- A career center. They help you figure out what to do with the rest of your life.

Kelly Schroeder, junior, University of Kansas, Lawrence

Seeing the whole campus. When you visit as a high school student, you only see a little part of it.

Lisa Moody, freshman, University of Nebraska–Omaha

DID WE MENTION THAT ...

They probably won't tell you this at orientation:
- How early you have to arrive at a huge lecture class to grab a seat where you can hear and see.
- Administrative assistants and desk attendants can give you helpful information.
- Where the best coffee kiosk is.
- How to stay awake during a seriously boring class.
- You'll never catch up on sleep.
- Where the nonorientation-sanctioned parties are that week.

Parent Orientation (No Kidding!)

During orientation and parents' weekend, it's like gourmet food. My folks said, "Wow! I sent three kids off to college and this is the only university I've seen with such good food!" But when your folks leave, it's macaroni-and-cheese, pasta, quesadillas. Nothing but carbs.
Shakira Ali, sophomore, Loyola University, Chicago

My parents went to a ton of meetings they said were really helpful. I'm the oldest, so my going to college was nerve-racking for them.
Rachel Pfennig, freshman, DePauw University, Greencastle, IN

My parents were bored at orientation, but then, I'm the second child to go to Cal-Tech and they already knew everything.
Marie Giron, freshman, California Institute of Technology, Pasadena

DID WE MENTION THAT ...

Many 18-year-olds would prefer their parents be invisible and if not, at least silent. Still, the 18-year-olds don't want to be left alone in the quad with all those strangers. And parents don't really want to say good-bye and leave their youngster alone in the quad with all those strangers. At orientation, that parent-child thing seems to click, which just proves you can do anything for a day or two.

Parents ask, "Where do students eat? Where are there quiet places to study?" You'll ask, "Where are the vending machines? Where's the pool hall?" Also, they pick up on financial stuff you would never think of. Like you have to have insurance or they won't let you register for classes.

Elizabeth Pitruzzello, senior, Central Connecticut State University, New Britain

On Mondays, anyone can visit TCU, talk with administrators and professors, ask students what they think. My mom did the Monday thing to make sure I would like my new environment. That was helpful for me.

Jeff Eskew, senior, Texas Christian University, Fort Worth

GET THIS! YOUR FRESHMAN LIFE—AND BEYOND

For some, coming to college will be a growing experience; for others, it will be a growing disaster. The social adjustment, being away from home for the first time, a roommate from a different culture, the workload, the I-don't-have-to-go-to-class-if-I-don't-want-to thing, newfound freedom as far as binge drinking or drugs—it's all there.

Adam Berry, senior, Emory University, Atlanta

GET THIS! HELICOPTER PARENTS

A growing number of parents hover, like helicopters, over their college student's life, micromanaging it toward perfection. We heard of one parent who even phoned her student with a wake-up call every day. Parent orientation meetings suggest appropriate ways for parents to still be part of their student's life while allowing the student space to develop skills for independence and success.

If you have HPs, you can help them let go by doing the following:

- Creating your own class schedule. Yes, it means reading about classes and requirements ahead of time.
- Not calling home daily and asking them not to call you, either. Some students call only for money or care packages. Surely you can find the middle ground.
- Not mentioning problems with classes or friends unless they present a danger to you or others.
- Saying, "No, thanks," as painful as it is, when your mom wants to come clean your room and do your laundry.
- Telling them you'll be (a) embarrassed, (b) insulted, (c) angry, or (d) all of the above if they call your professor if you fail a test.

Parents were there the three days of orientation. They had meetings and kept busy, too, but there was downtime so we could see them. It was an easing away rather than a "cold turkey" leaving. I think it helped my parents.

Beth Giudicessi, senior, University of Notre Dame (IN)

Homesick Blues

Suddenly it's time to say good-bye to everybody and everything you know, and that's scary. You don't want anything to change while you're gone. But everything will—especially you—and home will never again be quite the same. Fortunately, almost everyone else you'll meet is going through the same transition. They, too, are finding new friends while fending off homesickness, a very real problem that can strike in the first two minutes, two hours, two months—and can last two semesters. But it's not incurable, and as you test new experiences—stimulating classes, joining at least one activity, bonding with new friends, partying—you will find your niche.

Saying Good-bye: Tears, Fears, and Cheers

At first, leaving home is a terrifying thought. Your future is surrounded by the unknown. You are leaving your comfort zone, but with that, you will notice you have matured more.

Aaron Castro, junior, United States Naval Academy, Annapolis, MD

See every relative who is close by, even if only for five minutes. Make sure young cousins, brothers, and sisters know you are only going to be gone for a little while. They might think you're not coming back.

Ben Petersen, freshman, Northern Arizona University, Flagstaff

I told my family I loved them and was glad for everything they'd done for me. It wasn't easy, but it also wasn't hard because it was the truth. Don't hold back. You never know what can happen, even before you go home for Thanksgiving or Christmas break.

Will Burton, junior, University of Oregon, Eugene

On the ride to college, avoid conflict. You don't want people to leave with a sour taste in their mouths.

Ross Kaplan, senior, Colby College, Waterville, ME

When I finally said good-bye to my parents, I was bracing for strong emotion, but I had no idea how strong. We said good-bye in our hotel room, and all three of us broke down crying. It was even more powerful because my dad doesn't cry.

Erin Pirruccello, sophomore, University of Pennsylvania, Wharton School, Philadelphia

I was the last to leave of my friends, so I got to see everyone pack, took a lot of pictures, gave pictures to friends, and watched them go. You have to live for the present and don't project for when you will part.

Katie Beno, freshman, Gonzaga University, Spokane, WA

DID WE MENTION THAT . . .

After nine months of senioritis, a summer of "Don't-tell-me-what-to-do-because-I'm-an-adult!" coupled with the "Can-I-have-$20-to-go-out-with-my-friends?" plea, your parents are actually happy to send you off—but leaving you at school is something else.

As you watch their car drive away, you begin to realize how much you appreciate things your parents did or said that you had taken for granted.

Sage Middleton, senior, Tulane University, New Orleans

I couldn't wait for my parents to leave because then I would be completely independent. You can go hop on your bed and the only person who might be upset is the person underneath your bed.

Katie Loberg, junior, Loyola University, Chicago

GET THIS! HEADING HOME ALREADY?

Before leaving home, coordinate your first weekend visit home with family and friends. Allowing the trip to become the focal point of your life, though, means you're focusing on home, not school. Same for running home every weekend: You can't give your new life a shot if you're never around to live it.

Missing Your Dog, Your Mother, Your Room, and Your Parents' Car

A lot of kids were happy to leave high school. Not me. I *knew* high school, but I didn't know college.

Chelsea Chaney, junior, Washburn University, Topeka, KS

What I missed really was that when I was in high school, I knew a lot of people. At college, I walked down the street and there were no faces I knew. Even with all those people, I felt lonely.

Martha Edwards, senior, Marquette University, Milwaukee

It's easy to keep in touch with those who you really care about through IM, e-mails, and cell phones. My high school friends are as close, if not closer, than we were before college.

Jenn Mulroe, senior, University of Connecticut, Storrs

20/20 HINDSIGHT

Everybody goes away, does exciting things, comes back, and shares them with each other. So that good-bye thing was bigger than it needed to be.

Christine Fletcher, junior, Bates College, Lewiston, ME

The first month, I got stressed out because my mom forgot to pay the phone bill, my new computer broke, and there was no way to get hold of anyone, so then I felt a bit homesick. It was a long 24 hours until my phone was reinstated. My roommate helped a lot.

Jessica Monroe, sophomore, Butler University, Indianapolis

I'm only about two hours away but I didn't go home first semester until Thanksgiving. That was kind of hard. You have a lot more time in college so you have to find things to do and keep yourself occupied. It will pass.

Olamide Oduyingbo, freshman, Quinnipiac University, Hamden, CT

My sophomore roommate only lived an hour away from school, so her boyfriend picked her up every weekend and took her home. She really missed out on college life.

Anonymous

DID WE MENTION THAT ...

Parents like to be called. But remember:
1. Your parents are asleep at 1 A.M.
2. It will take them awhile to realize you are asleep at 8 A.M. And 9 A.M. Eventually, they won't call before noon.
3. E-mails don't count. Neither do text messages.

I was not homesick. I live only an hour away, but I've never been that kind of kid. I saw college as, okay, I am on my own now.

Jennifer Herlihy, senior, University of California–Berkeley

Surround yourself with people who make you laugh. Positive energy takes your mind off the missing factor. And, of course, it is always okay to cry.

Jackie Kohler, sophomore, Mercyhurst College, Erie, PA

GET THIS! LOBBY FOR YOUR CARE PACKAGE

▶ Tell the folks *everyone* is getting care packages—snacks, gift cards to Target, iTunes, and Best Buy, magazines, Halloween and Valentine's Day decorations, homemade cookies, vitamins, a flashlight, DVDs, and boxers. You can mention that your friends also get shoe boxes stuffed with money, but unless your parents are exceptionally gullible, that probably won't fly.

A week or two into school I was feeling kind of lonely and frustrated with life here. Even though I'm not very religious, I went to see the chaplain-in-residence, who was the first person I had met the first day on the way to my dorm. Then a friend at home committed suicide and the chaplain-in-residence was very considerate, a good listener, and we talked weekly.

Clark Young, freshman, Georgetown University, Washington, DC

▶ It's good to have friends who have cars and come from your hometown.

Will Burton, junior, University of Oregon, Eugene

Not having a car is really tough. You see the same scenery three weeks in a row until you talk someone into giving you a ride down to Wal-Mart—the highlight of the month.

Ande Davis, senior, Washburn University, Topeka, KS

GET THIS! HERE'S WHAT I MISSED

• Big sinks. The sinks here were so small that when you were washing your face you had to make sure your face didn't hit the faucet.

Martha Edwards, senior, Marquette University, Milwaukee

• My big bed, my big room, and I don't have a vacuum.

Sandra Lazo de la Vega, sophomore, Florida Atlantic University, Wilkes Honors College, Jupiter

• Our shower. I hated wearing sandals and having to walk through the halls to get to the shower in the dorm. We had four showers for 20 people.

Tyler Sloss, sophomore, Duke University, Durham, NC

• A set schedule. At first, college seemed to be a total free-for-all—from going out on a Tuesday night to sleeping until noon on a Thursday.

Jenn Mulroe, senior, University of Connecticut, Storrs

• Home-cooked meals. Nothing beats Grandma's cooking.

Shelly Haffner, sophomore, University of Wisconsin–Oshkosh

Homesickness—It's Real

You'll be homesick for the first three hours. But the first week on campus they have so many activities for incoming freshmen to meet new people. And if all else fails, you have your roommate!

Katie Jozwik, junior, Columbia College, Chicago

GET THIS! THREE THINGS YOU'LL BE GLAD TO LEAVE BEHIND

1. High school cliques because, thankfully, they just don't matter anymore.
2. All those excuses for why you overslept and understudied, again. Your roommate is too busy oversleeping and understudying to care.
3. Clean laundry that magically appears, folded, on your bed once a week. Oh, wait! You'd *like* to bring that with you.

I was quite homesick for the first week or so. Then I realized that I was having a great time! I was meeting new people, enjoying a new city, and I could go home (2½ hours away) any weekend I wanted!

Claire K. Harris, junior, Vanderbilt University, Nashville, TN

I got homesick after that first month or two, even though I was in a routine and had new friends. You think you've adjusted but you haven't completely. Call your friends from home. It helps.

Lauren Press, junior, University of Denver

First semester is going to be hard. You are figuring things out. Go or not go? Do or not do? Give yourself a chance to adjust by staying the whole year. College isn't bad, just different.

Sage Middleton, senior, Tulane University, New Orleans

I was homesick as a freshman. Now, summer's almost over and I'm going back as a sophomore and, yeah, I feel homesick again. I'll just make the best of the time I have here at home.

Tyler Sloss, sophomore, Duke University, Durham, NC

I wasn't homesick until the beginning of November. At first, it was so warm and I was making friends, partying, excited to be in college. Then the leaves started to change. I missed my street, my city, my fall experience. My best friend went home one weekend and took pictures and it just broke my heart, so I went home the next weekend.

Katia Porzecanski, sophomore, Tufts University, Medford, MA

The first four months of school were so exciting. I was partying, talking with my roommates, trying restaurants, doing everything new that I don't do at home. Then after first-semester midterms, it really hit and all I wanted to do was just go home.

Laura Polden, freshman, George Washington University, Washington, DC

It's second semester and I still miss home. I got a text message from my younger sister that she was sad because of something going on in her life. I don't think she would have ever shared that with me except that I was so far away. I miss being a member of my family because I'm not contributing to whatever is going on with them.

Clark Young, freshman, Georgetown University, Washington, DC

DID WE MENTION THAT . . .

Believe it: ignoring homesickness might register as fatigue, headaches, or upset stomachs, or even leave you feeling unmotivated. If you are so homesick that functioning socially and academically seems to slip from your grasp, run, don't walk, and talk to your R.A., a counselor, the health center nurse/doctor, a professor, a dean, your roommates—anyone and everyone until someone can help you.

I definitely wish I had known, understood, or accepted that not every day was going to be a big party. That would have helped me be real to the emotions I was feeling rather than ignoring them until they became almost unmanageable. It's okay to have bad days and to be sad and to miss your family and to want to be home.

Angela Kinney, freshman, Saint Louis University, St. Louis, MO

I've seen this *many* times: *do not* hang on to your friends from home to the point that you disable yourself from making new ones. This makes homesickness *much* worse.

Amie Reed, junior, Illinois State University, Normal

The worst time for homesickness is two weeks leading up to break.

Brittany Borstad, junior, Iowa State University, Ames

20/20 HINDSIGHT

Going from [a midwestern city] to West Philadelphia was quite a culture shock. I wasn't expecting how challenging it would be—the change in lifestyle as well as going to college. The biggest difference was the people, their ways of approaching life, such a faster pace of life. Here, I'm inclined to walk slowly, but friends are more likely to hurry. At home, people are more open, down to earth, and friendly; here, so many people just want to get through their day. I'm not bashing the culture; it's just different.

Erin Pirruccello, sophomore, University of Pennsylvania, Wharton School, Philadelphia

GET THIS! TESTED AND APPROVED REMEDIES FOR HOMESICKNESS

- You don't have to announce it to the entire dining hall, but admit to yourself that you're really homesick.
- Go for coffee with your roommate and talk about *anything* but being homesick.
- Get yourself out to Ultimate Frisbee, flag football, yoga or martial arts classes—any activity for instant action that will give you an exercise-induced endorphin high.
- Eat meals that aren't fried in batter and served off a dollar menu. Oh, and get some sleep. Crappy food and not enough rest affect you every which way but good.
- Say "Hi" to the guy in your Spanish class or the girl who lives down the hall. Most likely you'll get a "hi" back. Simple, right?
- List all the stuff your parents told you not to do. Then do the legal stuff.

When you are at school, be at school and when you are home, be at home. Don't think about school when you are home, and don't think about home when you are at school.

Rachel Lenz, junior, Vassar College, Poughkeepsie, NY

20/20 HINDSIGHT

I was excited to leave small-town life and experience life on a huge campus in a city where you can't drive down the street and wave to everybody. Even so, the night before I left, I was crying. It took like about a month to get okay. I had sophomore roommates who'd been through this, conversations with my family, and got busy with homework. Then I didn't have time to think about how things had changed. Second semester, I only went home twice, and thought, "I want to go back to school."

Lisa Moody, freshman, University of Nebraska–Omaha

Looking for Those New Best Friends

I didn't find my ideal group of friends the week I arrived, and I wondered if Harvard was not exactly what I wanted it to be. It might even take a full year before you have your perfect niche.

Christina Hoffman, junior, Harvard University, Cambridge, MA

Even at a school as small as Williams, you aren't going to know everyone, so as long as you don't do anything extremely heinous, you're probably in the clear to act as crazy as you want.

Allison McAndrew, sophomore, Williams College, Williamstown, MA

You're stuck in a dorm with 100 strangers, so you meet them and judge later. It's easy to think, "That person's in that fraternity so he must be this way" and, "That person's an athlete so she must be this way." Snap judgments close you off to other people.

Elizabeth Joyce, sophomore, Stanford (CA) University

Keep an open mind. That was especially important for me coming from a small town. Within days I met so many people with different ways of life and attitudes. Most turned into amazing friends. Now I just enjoy meeting as many people as possible. That makes every day at a school of 40,000 students exciting.

Chris Petz, senior, University of Washington, Seattle

I was wearing a T-shirt that had *The X-Files* on it, and another girl started talking about that show. Don't be afraid to strike up conversation on common ground.

Leverett Woodruff, sophomore, Westminster College, Salt Lake City

> Popularity doesn't matter. As long as you understand that everyone is weird, then you'll know that everyone is normal and everyone fits in.
>
> *Colleen Johnson, freshman, Webster University, St. Louis, MO*

GET THIS! HOW TO BE AN INSTANT CELEBRITY

The first month of school, I was standing on a desk at midnight to hang something on the wall, and as I stepped down, I crashed to the ground, hitting my head, twisting my ankle, and hitting my toes at an odd angle. I was freaking out, so a friend called our emergency service. By the time they got there, I had realized my leg was fine, but since I was under 18, they had to take me to the hospital anyway—for a stubbed toe! The X-rays cost my mom a couple hundred dollars. But I was a celebrity for, like, a week.

Alix Lifka-Reselman, freshman, Brandeis University, Waltham, MA

> It's easy in college to meet boys. They visit you when you move into the dorm. It's harder to meet girls, but they're the ones you'll be friends with.
>
> Chelsea Chaney, junior, Washburn University, Topeka, KS

Notice what kinds of friends you're making: Are your friends self-centered? Fun? A constant drag? Why are you attracted to these kinds of people, and is that a good thing? You learn the most about yourself in the kind of friends you make.

Luke Roth, freshman, Loyola University, Chicago

Keep your door open, cell phone off, and laptop closed. Sounds like a big commitment, but if you are the homesick person—and I was Mr. Homesick my entire life—it's amazing how you will meet people.

Zack Barr, freshman, Brandeis University, Waltham, MA

Making friends in college is different than at home. When you are telling a story in college, you must tell all this back-story because people don't know you.

Martha Edwards, senior, Marquette University, Milwaukee

GET THIS! PRESSING TOO HARD

> I knew someone who checked her e-mail like it was her job. She'd press other people to make plans to hang out the next day. People stopped talking to her.
>
> Lori Donovan, junior, St. Olaf College, Northfield, MN

20/20 **HINDSIGHT**

Getting past the fear of speaking to new people is the first and most crucial step. It took me a good semester and a half of living alone to realize a simple truth: Most of the other students are as unsure, lonely, and as willing to meet new people as you. After that, I began random conversations with just about anybody, and most of those strangers ended up becoming my friends.

Leor Benyamini, junior, Quinnipiac University, Hamden, CT

Facebook—Pervasive Procrastination Tool?

We say a person who lists 500 friends is a Facebook whore.
Ben Petersen, freshman, Northern Arizona University, Flagstaff

It's a huge procrastination tool and tends to be very addictive. You find yourself searching for everyone you've ever known so you can add them to your friends list.
Caitlin Wells, junior, Grinnell (IA) College

It's like reading someone's diary, looking at their stuff without them knowing it. It's kind of like stalking.
Sage Middleton, senior, Tulane University, New Orleans

Facebook generates questions. Like, "Do you think it's weird that a lot of kids list 110 college friends before they even arrive on campus?"
Paul Bromen, junior, St. Olaf College, Northfield, MN

GET THIS! FIVE SUREFIRE WAYS TO MAKE FRIENDS

1. Never start a conversation with "I miss my parents."
2. Invite people to screen movie classics in your room. Yes, *Caddyshack* is considered a classic.
3. Do not tuck your shirt into pleated pants. Better yet, do not wear pleated pants.
4. Get to your 2 A.M. hall barbecue.
5. Bring random games from home, like Nintendo 64 that nobody's played since eighth grade.

There are random people who ask to be friends. If you know them at all, you usually accept them, but some people just want another response for their list.

Katharine McCormick, sophomore, University of Pennsylvania, Philadelphia

Facebook can be mildly useful, for example, in coming up with gift ideas. ("What CD should I get her for her birthday? Let's check out her favorite bands!")

Michael Salvati, junior, Villanova University, Philadelphia, PA

BELIEVE IT! SIBLING-STRANGERS MEET ON FACEBOOK

My brother found me through Facebook. I didn't know I had a brother. Last year he sent me a message saying, "I think you're my sister." Everything turned out a lot better than it seems to on talk shows. He and I have bonded even though we live across the country from one another.

Jennifer Herlihy, senior, University of California–Berkeley

Either you have a profile or you think it is really stupid.

Becca Strutt, senior, Hope College, Holland, MI

If in your profile you list "smokin' blunts while beer bonging" as an interest and even have pictures documenting you doing so, potential employers might not look so favorably upon this. If you absolutely must include incriminating information and/or pictures to show off to your friends, make sure your profile is private and/or use a name or moniker that won't be easily recognized. The "un-tag" feature of pictures posted by others may also prove to be a great friend.

Tien Nguyen, senior, University of California–Los Angeles

DID WE MENTION THAT . . .

You probably have more privacy wrapped in a towel on the way to the shower than you do on the Internet. Out of curiosity we Googled a student we know, looking for the student's blog. Instead, we found other bloggers who had written about the student's use of an illegal substance. The student was identified by full name, city, and high school. Such entries hang around long after you've cut out any experimentation or habits.

Oops, That Friendship Didn't Work Out

I thought we would be good friends, but she talked to me about other people, and I realized she was talking to them about me. I dealt with the hurt by talking with my folks. Eventually, she left school. You have to say, what's in the past is in the past and just move on.

Lisa Moody, freshman, University of Nebraska–Omaha

Partying is probably not the best way to make friends. At first, everyone is going out and getting drunk. That heart-to-heart you have with someone at 3 A.M. may be less consequential than you thought at the time.

Christina Hoffman, junior, Harvard University, Cambridge, MA

Friendships change sophomore year from your freshman year.

Rachel Lenz, junior, Vassar College, Poughkeepsie, NY

20/20 HINDSIGHT

I bonded with a guy at orientation because we had the same sense of humor. But as we got to know each other, our friendship gradually and naturally fell by the wayside. At first, you're just reaching out and grasping for immediate friendships; you make rash judgments like, "Oh, my gosh, she is going to be my best friend!" As you start making friends based on common interests, those friendships fade.

Emily Gravett, senior, Colgate University, Hamilton, NY

How to Spend an Entire Parents' Weekend with Your Parents

I specifically asked my parents to come and loved going to dinner and sightseeing with them. It was hard because there were lots of exams near that time, so I wondered how I was going to divide the time. But it worked out.

Erin Pirruccello, sophomore, University of Pennsylvania, Wharton School, Philadelphia

They came up for Parents' Weekend, sat in on one of my classes, had no idea what the teacher was saying, and I knew everything. They have no idea what I know.

Jason Kaplan, senior, Colgate University, Hamilton, NY

Make sure your folks realize that you won't want to stay with them 24/7. After dinner, they can go back to the hotel and you can go out. Some parents want to be kids again. They join in the drinking games and you have to beat them at beer pong. I'm glad my parents aren't like that.

Graham Shepherd, senior, DePauw University, Greencastle, IN

GET THIS! THINGS TO SAY TO THE PARENTS

- "I'll show you my favorite place to read in the library."
- "I'd like to come back to the hotel with you after dinner, but I've got a ton of homework."
- "Thanks, but I can't think of a single thing you need to buy for me."
- "Parties? Here? Not really."

GET THIS! THINGS *NOT* TO SAY TO THE PARENTS

- "It's like summer camp here all the time!"
- "Professors don't care if you don't show up for your 8 o'clock class."
- "Everyone calls this the party dorm, but there's another one that's way worse."
- "I hooked up at my very first party! Twice!"

It was the most horrible rainy weather, Jon Stewart performed on campus, and all the parents and kids came. Maybe I was just PMS-y, but I was in the worst mood. I'd come into our room and it would be packed with people. I wished my mom and aunt had come a different weekend so we could just chill and see what GW is like without GW being all gussied up—they gussy up because we're paying $50,000 a year so they want it to look good.

Laura Polden, freshman, George Washington University, Washington, DC

I had my parents see every inch of the campus. After that, they really entertained themselves with a Revolutionary War tour.

Katia Porzecanski, sophomore, Tufts University, Medford, MA

Sometimes, having parents visit can be a little overbearing. Like when they're in your room trying to clean up, or you have a paper due and they want to go out somewhere. Just go with the flow. They're only there a couple days.

Harrison Macris, sophomore, Boston University

DID WE MENTION THAT . . .

▶ Dining halls are known to notch up the food quality for special events, including Parents' Weekend. It almost makes you wish they had Parents' Weekend every month, doesn't it.

Going Home: Your Old Life Doesn't Fit the New You

My room at home is preserved, if you will. My books. Pictures. Except now there's dog hair all over the bed. He's kind of taken over.

Graham Shepherd, senior, DePauw University, Greencastle, IN

You'll love going back home for comfort things, like sleeping in your own bed, hanging out in your house in sweatpants and doing nothing.

Christine Fletcher, junior, Bates College, Lewiston, ME

Going back home is awkward. Part of it is you haven't kept in touch with your old friends, and part is you underestimate how much you've grown as a person in the first months of college.

Scott Beggs, senior, Baylor University, Waco, TX

At first it was weird going home. Mom wanted a kind of curfew. But they didn't have any control. It was useless to try to change rules I had at college. Here I can stay out all night.

Diane Hennan, freshman, Saint Ambrose University, Davenport, IA

DID WE MENTION THAT . . .

> Your folks already know you've changed, and they're a little
> nervous for this visit. Be kind.

When I got back for Christmas *everything* changed—no curfew, family
would offer drinks with meals, and finally being listened to as an adult!

Sarah Kiener, freshman, Catholic University of America, Washington, DC

A lot of us had been growing apart senior year, but we stayed together
because we were a group. When I came home for break, I saw only
the people I wanted to see. It was weird—when you do that, it's
different and you don't have as many friends.

Zack Barr, freshman, Brandeis University, Waltham, MA

I came home for Thanksgiving and everything in the house was changed
and I had emotional problems with that. All the walls were white when
I left, and my mom went crazy and painted walls everywhere all
different colors—purple, mustard, blue. . . .

Laura Polden, freshman, George Washington University, Washington, DC

You have a lot you want to talk about but realize you don't have
anything to say because it's almost, like, too very different. Like that
Neil Diamond song, "New York's home but it ain't mine no more,"
I love my city, but I didn't feel like it was my home anymore because
I knew it would be a long time before I was back there again.

Clark Young, freshman, Georgetown University, Washington, DC

Some of your family won't get it that you've been living away from home. They'll question you about where you're going and for how long. My grandpa did that, and then he said, "You're just growing up and I don't think I wanted you to."

Leverett Woodruff, sophomore, Westminster College, Salt Lake City

GET THIS! HOME-AGAIN STRATEGIES

- Skip falling back into the role you played in high school. That's like wearing the clothes you got in tenth grade.
- Don't talk to your old friends about how great your new friends are.
- Remind yourself that a week at home in no way resembles a week at a spa.
- Even if you're insanely popular on campus, you're still "just you" at home.
- Announce early what time you are going back to school so the parents don't plan a big Sunday-evening dinner with all the relatives when you plan to leave at noon.

My mom was convinced I couldn't survive, like I wouldn't put the $7 down for Tylenol. I convinced her I'd take Tylenol if she'd pay for it. Go home, stock up on Tylenol, snacks and, every once in a while, clothes.

Mike Husni, junior, University of Delaware, Newark

GET THIS! ADRIENNE'S STORY: YOU CAN'T GO HOME AGAIN ... TO YOUR BEDROOM

Right after I left, my sister moved into my bedroom and my brother took her room, leaving me the smallest bedroom during winter break. Second semester, my mom calls and says, "Hey, Adrienne, we are going to turn your room into an office. Would you like to set up a bedroom in the laundry room or the basement?" I reluctantly, and complainingly, took a makeshift bedroom in the basement for that summer. And then I come home for sophomore winter break and guess what my brother got for his Christmas present? A *ping-pong table*. And they wanted to set it up (in the basement) before I went back to school! At spring break I went home for three days and slept on the couch. I guess I get the picture. I'm not moving back home—ever.

Adrienne May, sophomore, University of Missouri–Kansas City

Chapter 5

Roommates: Friends, Foes, or Somewhere in Between

This part of college life is a big deal. You move into what feels like a closet, hauling along all your stuff, including your Dave Matthews subway poster, and your roommate brings a kayak and your mom wants to help you unpack—and that's just the first hour. For the next nine months, you'll find out more than you ever wanted to know about your roommate and yourself. This learning and growing process will be fun, difficult, rewarding, depressing—sometimes as challenging as your toughest class. What gets you through? Patience, a willingness to listen, and a penchant for being nonjudgmental. When that's not possible, very thick skin and/or somebody to talk with should help. Ultimately, you might become best friends or merely people who sleep in the same room.

First Person in the Room Gets the Best Bed— Sometimes

I was the second person in and got the smaller room in the suite. So, yes, it's true.

Caitlin Wells, sophomore, Grinnell (IA) College

I got there a day earlier. I kind of wanted to stake claim, but as soon as she showed up I said, "We can move stuff around, do whatever you want."
Beth Giudicessi, senior, University of Notre Dame (IN)

If you're there first, claim the best bed, especially if you don't know your roommate. I think the other person would do the same. I don't want to step on toes, but that's how it is.

Chelsea Chaney, junior, Washburn University, Topeka, KS

I got to the room first, plopped everything down on the bed closest to the door, and that's how the decision was made. Nothing's really permanent anyway. We switched things around a couple of times.
Ross Kaplan, senior, Colby College, Waterville, ME

My roommate got there first. There was a crater the size of a meteor in the mattress I got. I don't know if she tested the mattresses and chose the other one or what. But she never did anything else that was selfish or greedy, so I didn't say anything.
Leverett Woodruff, sophomore, Westminster College, Salt Lake City

GET THIS! RAIJA'S REPORT ABOUT BUNK BEDS

There isn't such a thing as a best bed.

Downsides to the bottom bunk:

- You clunk your head on the supports under the top bunk if you sit up too quickly.
- People sit here when they come in your room.
- If someone gets sick and your room is open, they'll crawl into the bottom bunk because they can't make it to the top bunk.

Downsides to the top bunk:

- You need good eyesight to climb up in the dark.
- Climbing down in the morning is a pretty jarring way to wake up.
- If you're studying in bed and forget a book, it takes a lot more energy to grab it off your desk.

Raija Bushnell, freshman, DePauw University, Greencastle, IN

We decided who got what when we moved in. She got the top bunk, but she fell off one night, so we traded.

Joanna Stone, senior, University of Mississippi, Oxford

Movin' on In

When they say moving day, they mean moving *day*. Don't go with the skewed notion that moving in will take 30 minutes. Your parents will freak out more than you because they can't find a parking place, and their good-byes will take an hour. Even so, let them have their day of experiencing college all over again. That night, you can do whatever you want.

Katie Loberg, junior, Loyola University, Chicago

If your brothers and sisters can come, moving in is more fun. I wondered if I'd be the only person with her whole family along, but I wasn't.

Emily Cullings, junior, Colgate University, Hamilton, NY

It was somewhat sad because most students had their parents come help them move in, and I didn't have anyone there to help me. However, I met a lot more parents and students because they wanted to help me feel more at home.

Sri Kalyanaraman, junior, Brown University, Providence, RI

Moving in was complete chaos with hundreds of people unloading. A bed someone was moving in hit and broke the third-floor sprinkler and the bottom three floors had to be evacuated.

Brian Steimers, junior, University of Delaware, Newark

Bring your big brother along, in case you don't have an elevator. It's definitely a struggle lugging a futon up four flights of stairs.

Christina Hoffman, junior, Harvard University, Cambridge, MA

My father and I were
yelling at each other
putting up the loft
we'd brought. But
my dad and Allison's
dad talked a lot
about power drills;
the dads bonded.

Caitlin Wells, sophomore,
Grinnell (IA) College

DID WE MENTION THAT . . .

Lots of mothers will want to arrange things for you. Even when
you haven't asked for help. And don't want help. They think
it's their job.

It was really comforting that my mom made my bed.

Emily Cullings, junior, Colgate University, Hamilton, NY

My roommate's family drove to campus in 90 minutes. All the
commotion was being caused by *my* family, who had just been on a
six-hour, nonstop flight. I was afraid they'd think we were crazy. I

wanted my folks to go wait in a cab! But everybody helped unpack, and we all went to supper together.

Nikki Hasbun, freshman, University of Notre Dame (IN)

We got everything into the room, pieced it all together, and made it fit. But it didn't last, and pretty soon, we had to get bed risers so we could set more things under the beds.

Will Burton, junior, University of Oregon, Eugene

At home, you were doing your own thing and having stuff the way you wanted it. Now, you're thrown in with people not familiar to you. You'll learn to be more patient.

Harrison Macris, sophomore, Boston University

My friend suggested we flip the mattress because of the dust that had been accumulating on it over the summer. There was a bright red thong on the other side! I guess it was a remnant of last year's tenants' adventures.

Antha Mack, freshman, University of California– San Diego

20/20 HINDSIGHT

Move in as quickly as possible. People who stretch out unpacking and getting settled for a week or so make themselves miserable. Then, move off campus as soon as you can so you have some room.

James Langlois, junior, Tulane University, New Orleans

Getting to Know You

If you're always worrying about being friends with your roommate, you won't be yourself.

Christine Fletcher, junior, Bates College, Lewiston, ME

My roommate brought a TV and classic movies to share. It's an easy way to get to know each other.

Bryn Rouse, sophomore, University of Montana, Missoula

The first night, even though I already had really, really good guy friends on campus, I made it a point to go out to eat with my new roommate.

Joanna Stone, senior, University of Mississippi, Oxford

GET THIS! ROOMMATE FIRST-LINERS YOU DO *NOT* WANT TO HEAR

- "My boyfriend from high school lives one floor down. We fight a lot but we make up a lot, too, if you know what I mean."
- "I hope our room will be a quiet place. I value quiet."
- "I'm a total party person. Sometimes I drink too much, but hey, this is college."

My roommate and I stayed up late talking from almost the first night. In the beginning, it was about likes and dislikes. But it moved to helping each other through bad days and sharing dreams. I was surprised at the bonding.

Rosie M. Gregg, sophomore, Baylor University, Waco, TX

DID WE MENTION THAT . . .

> You've never shared a bedroom in your whole life and suddenly, you and a complete stranger are in this room the size of a broom closet, getting ready for bed, and everyone is acting like this is normal, which it is not. The only thing "normal" is that you're both nervous.

We talked about our take on nudity. I went to an all-girls school, and after that, you don't care about being naked around other girls. I wasn't sure how she would feel, but it turns out she's been around water polo teams all her life. So it didn't bother her, either.

Antha Mack, freshman, University of California–San Diego

My roommate was a stranger from Hawaii, and we got along really well even though we didn't hang out. We set guidelines like not wanting friends in the room when either of us was studying. She'd feed my fish when I went out of town.

Colleen Thurston, junior, University of Arizona, Tucson

Don't worry if you and your roommate are total opposites. You won't be together every single minute of every single day.

Courtney Kelley, freshman, University of Iowa, Iowa City

20/20 HINDSIGHT

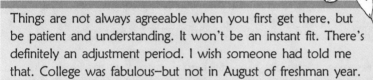

Things are not always agreeable when you first get there, but be patient and understanding. It won't be an instant fit. There's definitely an adjustment period. I wish someone had told me that. College was fabulous—but not in August of freshman year.

Amanda Vazzano, senior, Miami University, Oxford, OH

Hang out together. Have lunch together. But don't assume because you hit it off at first that you are going to be best friends.

Henna Messina, senior, Fordham University, New York

Your roommate doesn't always end up being your bridesmaid.

Angela Kinney, freshman, Saint Louis University, St. Louis, MO

The first night, my buddy and I tried to get familiar with the campus. This guy yelled at us from his front porch, "Hey, are you freshmen? Come on in." There was a huge party, hundreds of people, 90 percent freshmen. The upperclassmen were real welcoming, not like when you first go to high school and upperclassmen don't want to have anything to do with you.

Brian Steimers, junior, University of Delaware, Newark

My roommate ended up leaving, so I had no roommate for about a month, which was pretty miserable. Don't necessarily wish for a single, because it's lonely freshman year. You don't have a partner in crime to go out and explore with.

Cristina Baptista, graduate student, Fordham University, Bronx, NY

DID WE MENTION THAT . . .

▶ If you bring a toolkit, you'll meet everybody on your floor sooner or later.

My freshman roommate came to school, picked up the keys, left, and never came back. The school couldn't find her for months, so I had a single for the first semester. It worked out great because I hung out with friends on another floor, and when my boyfriend came to visit, we had the room to ourselves.

Anonymous

First semester my roommate was in the shower and the fire alarm went off. She had to go out and stand on the lawn in her towel. You're trying to impress people and you look like a wet dog and you're mortified. I came home from class and looked for her and she's standing there pissed off.

Laura Polden, freshman, George Washington University, Washington, DC

20/20 **HINDSIGHT**

Really know your roommate before you start letting him use your stuff. My friend's roommate took his car without permission and wrecked it.

Jeff Eskew, senior, Texas Christian University, Fort Worth

Three's a Crowd? It Depends . . .

Honestly, living with two roommates was like getting three five-year-olds to pick one type of ice cream. There are so many different flavors!

Courtney Fowlkes, sophomore, Baylor University, Waco, TX

With three in a suite, you'll like one more than the other, and end up talking to each other about the things that annoy you about the third roommate. That's bad, but worse if you're the third roommate.

Brittany Borstad, junior, Iowa State University, Ames

I'm in a suite with five other girls from Seattle. Kids from Seattle have a totally different view of life than a kid from the Midwest.

Katie Beno, freshman, Gonzaga University, Spokane, WA

The number one rule on food and multiple roommates is either all pitch in and share the cost and share the food, or everyone gets his own food and others don't eat it.

Leor Benyamini, junior, Quinnipiac University, Hamden, CT

The toughest relationship on campus is between you and your roommate's girlfriend. She becomes the third member of your room and you didn't really get to choose. If you tease people, never do that to her.

Paul Bromen, junior, St. Olaf College, Northfield, MN

GET THIS! FOUR CONVERSATION DUDS

1. "Actually, I've never met *anybody* from your part of the country."
2. "So, how many schools accepted you?"
3. "I was on the homecoming court and student council and in the orchestra and ran track and . . ."
4. "You're still a virgin? Weird."

Rooming with Your High School Friend

It's Awesome!

The transition was easier because I knew I was going to have at least one friend on campus. We did so much together that sometimes people would mistake us for twins.

Molly Olson, senior, Iowa State University, Ames

Wait until you're an upperclassman and more mature to live with your friend. You'll know how to handle each other's differences by then.

Anna Skelly, senior, California State University–Long Beach

Before you decide to room together, go on a road trip together. If you get annoyed by even a couple of little things after a six-hour road trip, you might not want to live with that person for a year.

Alan Kistler, senior, Fordham University, New York

Before you decide to room together, sit down and talk about potential room scenarios. For example, if the trash is full and you have more trash, would you pile yours on top or take it all out to the Dumpster? If you wanted to have friends over, would you ask if it's okay or just do it? If you don't agree on the answers, you shouldn't be roommates.

Colleen Thurston, junior, University of Arizona, Tucson

DID WE MENTION THAT . . .

> Students tell us that to make the friends-as-roommates thing work, you need to act more like adults than teenagers.

Decide in advance whether you are on similar levels as far as cleanliness, drinking, and party habits–especially if you are sharing a really, really small space with a few square inches to walk around in.

James Langlois, junior, Tulane University, New Orleans

20/20 HINDSIGHT

I asked a high school friend to be my roommate. I'm liberal arts (theater); he's math. Having two very different people together might be the key. If I had roomed with my theater people, I probably would want to kill them.

Mike Husni, junior, University of Delaware, Newark

It's Awful!

We were more like friendly acquaintances. We knew what to expect, but we got tired of each other faster because of that. If I could do it over, I'd go with a randomly assigned roommate. There's an off chance you would become lifelong friends.

Will Burton, junior, University of Oregon, Eugene

Think you know your best friend? What time does he go to bed? Get up? Will he bring in outside friends and still be considerate of you? You don't really know. A better alternative is to get in the same dorm. Then you and your best friend will have two sets of new friends and you'll be building this network.

Jeff Eskew, senior, Texas Christian University, Fort Worth

How *Not* to Drive Each Other Crazy

At the beginning of the semester we had to sign a room contract. We had to answer questions like, "If there is an altercation, how will you handle it?" We set up times for going to bed and basically anticipated problems and how to solve them. It prevented us from screaming at each other.

Amanda Vazzano, senior, Miami University, Oxford, OH

We all laid down ground rules, including washing dishes as soon as we used them. But one roommate wouldn't even bring his dishes from his room to the kitchen. You can remind someone he's violating an agreement, but with some people, that doesn't matter.

Scott Beggs, senior, Baylor University, Waco, TX

Sharing everything works, if everyone agrees to that. There's no "you took my drink out of the fridge." What's mine is yours. We keep a mental tab of who gets the water and who gets the detergent this time and next time.

Graham Shepherd, senior, DePauw University, Greencastle, IN

I had a roommate who loved to eat all my food, then ask if it was all right.

Andrew Lack, senior, Iowa State University, Ames

When we first met, my roommate told me I was welcome to any of her food—except the Ring Dings. After that, I knew we'd get along.

Anonymous

20/20 HINDSIGHT

I didn't like living with one of my roommates, but after we stopped living together, we became friends. You can't always live with someone you like because of personal habits. But those habits don't matter in a friendship.

Henna Messina, senior, Fordham University, New York

Don't pretend you don't mind when your roommate bites his nails. Then it gets to the point where you snap and he doesn't understand why you are yelling at him.

Ben Petersen, freshman, Northern Arizona University, Flagstaff

Our biggest issue was she would get up at 5 A.M., put up the blinds, and use the printer.

Sarah Sentz, sophomore, University of Montana, Missoula

At a party is not the time to say to your roommate, "Hey, you didn't wash your dishes."

Alan Kistler, senior, Fordham University, New York

DID WE MENTION THAT . . .

Having the same sleeping patterns is way more important than the closet size. So we hear.

My roommate likes to play computer games all night and sleep all day. I'm now good at putting my contacts on in the dark.

Tanner Kokemuller, freshman, Colorado State University, Fort Collins

GET THIS! ROOMMATE-SPEAK IN THREE EASY STEPS

When (not if) your roommate is annoying:
1. Say, "Hey, I wouldn't even bring this up, except it *really* bugs me when such-and-such happens."
2. That's better than saying, "*You* do this and it bugs me."
3. End with, "Do you think we can work together?"

Leverett Woodruff, sophomore, Westminster College, Salt Lake City

My suitemate is a neat freak. I'm not. My bedroom is a dump, but I get an A+ for the communal space.

Anna Skelly, senior, California State University–Long Beach

GET THIS! A ROOMMATE RICHTER SCALE

How easy are you to live with? Respond with agree/disagree:
1. I believe the higher the volume, the better the music.
2. I never asked my sibling if I could borrow clothes, so I shouldn't have to ask my roommate, either.
3. I can bitch for an hour if you use my hair dryer. That's personal stuff.
4. Parties don't have to end. I can just bring beer and friends back to my place.

Try not to upset roommates, but don't let them encroach on your space. This is all temporary. The year will end and you will never have to live with them again.

Rebecca Zwisler, senior, St. Mary's College, Notre Dame, IN

To have a bedroom you could do whatever you please with is exciting—until you discover your roommate's lifestyle. I learned the importance of keeping my small area clean and always taking out the garbage. However, my roommate did not have a problem with leaving take-out containers on her desk for weeks at a time. That's when I wished someone came and checked our rooms.

Jenn Mulroe, senior, University of Connecticut, Storrs

When there is tension, find some common ground and hope everyone can give a little. My roommate and I had a time when we were not getting along and would just say, "Hi" and "Bye." Then she broke up with her boyfriend and needed someone to talk to. So we both let our guard down and broke the tension.

Beth Guidicessi, senior, University of Notre Dame (IN)

My biggest pet peeve about my roommate was that her thick, curly brown hair ended up everywhere. On the floor, on my clothes, blankets, you name it. It was the most disgusting thing in the world. If you have gross habits, clean them up before you get to school.

Brenna Derksen, freshman, University of Iowa, Iowa City

A lot of people have survival relationships where they coexist, are civil but they don't do stuff together and they don't get on each other's nerves.

Rachel Lenz, junior, Vassar College, Poughkeepsie, NY

20/20 HINDSIGHT

If the door is shut, it's probably for one of the three Big S's of college: sleeping, studying, sex. Wait until it's open again to go on in.

Jade Hidle, senior, California State University–Long Beach

The one hard thing to give up was my own space. When I am in my room alone—that happens about once a week—I watch the shows I want to, talk on the phone, sing, dance around, and listen to my music minus headphones.

Laura Polden, freshman, George Washington University, Washington, DC

If Things Get Really Bad

When one roommate thought I was sleeping, he'd go through stuff on my computer and desk. He didn't take anything, or if he did, I didn't realize it. Finally, I sat up and asked if I could help him with something. After that, we didn't talk much, but he didn't mess with my stuff. I spent as little time as possible in my room until the end of the semester. Since then, I've lived alone.

Jeff Eskew, senior, Texas Christian University, Fort Worth

GET THIS! USE YOUR ALONE TIME WISELY. PLEASE.

▶ Structure your masturbation schedule around your roommate's class schedule. We know a student who caught his roommate masturbating *all* the time because the guy does it when he thinks our student will be gone or sometimes when he thinks our student is sleeping. It's really awkward and our student hates it— says it's just one of the most discourteous things you can do.

BELIEVE IT! A ROOMMATE GOES POSTAL

▶ One student said his roommate barged in ranting, raving, and dripping wet from a swirlie. He plunged a screwdriver into the wall, yanked it back out, yelled that he was "going to kill those guys," and ran out. "He was always lying so I didn't know if this was a joke," our student said. "I just knew I'd better go after him." By the time he caught up with him, the roommate had pinned down another student and was punching his face. The screwdriver was on the floor beside them. Our student wrestled his roommate off while somebody got the R.A. Looking back, our student says the situation wasn't handled well. "The guy stayed my roommate all freshman year because I said he acted okay around me. My parents were really upset. Hey, I was only a freshman. I didn't know."

One roommate in our off-campus house did not flush the toilet, piled garbage on the full trash, and did not help clean our common areas. We all had a sit-down to talk about the situation and ask the roommate to pitch in. He refused and walked out of the meeting. After a couple of months, because I also owned the house, I told the roommate,

"You can't live here if you don't realize we aren't your housekeepers and take part in keeping the house clean." There was an uneasy truce, and things were better.

Leor Benyamini, junior, Quinnipiac University, Hamden, CT

I'd rather have a roommate who drinks and parties than one who doesn't do her laundry or shower. You think those roommate-from-hell stories aren't true, but I had one. She never did laundry freshman year. She'd go home on the weekends, but leave her laundry in the dorm. I ended up having to switch rooms. You have to have somebody hygienic.

Shakira Ali, sophomore, Loyola University, Chicago

Resident Assistants—All-Purpose Students

We're not police officers. Freshmen are shy, nervous when they first get to campus. They don't know how to take us, often seeing us as an enforcer of the rules rather than as a friend.

Matt Bielich, senior, R.A., University of California–San Diego

---

GET THIS! KNOCK ON YOUR R.A.'S DOOR IF . . .

- you wonder what some really good classes are or which professors to avoid;
- you want the skinny on which activities to join;
- you encounter gender or ethnic insensitivity or outright discrimination;
- you feel so homesick you could throw up;
- your roommate is heavy into drugs and alcohol. Or you are;
- your suitemate plays guitar at 2 A.M. (and isn't even good);
- your friend lives on coffee, carrots, and cigarettes and works out four times a day;
- your roommate confides that he or she has contemplated suicide.

The most general rule is you have to know when you can't handle a problem yourself and go to someone else. A lot of freshmen will live with problems in rooms or grades, sickness or mental sickness. They try to stick it out and make it go away. But if they will come to an R.A., who is specially trained, the R.A. will know what to do or who to send the person to.

Laura MacLean, senior, R.A., University of Notre Dame (IN)

20/20 HINDSIGHT

My roommate said I snored, even though other people said that was not a problem. She wouldn't wear earplugs, but insisted I wear sleep strips. If you see a situation affecting academics, talk to the R.A. I definitely should have done that. Instead, I ended up sleeping in a friend's room most of the first 10 weeks.

Marie Giron, freshman, California Institute of Technology, Pasadena

> **DID WE MENTION THAT . . .**
>
> R.A.s aren't about to be your parents in absentia. One freshman's parent, who had grounded the student before leaving for college, wanted the R.A. to continue the sanction by making sure the student stayed in the dorm room for the next week and wasn't allowed to use any phones. Didn't happen. R.A.s don't babysit.

Sex and the Double Room

If your roommate and his girl come in and you know there is any romantic interest, sex takes the highest priority. Get your ass out of there. Say, "Oh, hey, how are you crazy kids doing? I have to go to the library for two hours." Audibly say how much time you are going to give them.

Paul Bromen, junior, St. Olaf College, Northfield, MN

If there is going to be any interaction between male and female and you get kicked out of your room, we say you've been *sexiled*.

Raija Bushnell, freshman, DePauw University, Greencastle, IN

If the girlfriend-boyfriend thing makes you feel like you don't live in your own room anymore, there's a problem you need to talk about.

Scott Beggs, senior, Baylor University, Waco, TX

I was the one who didn't include my roommates when my boyfriend was there. You might not feel bad at the time if no one complains.

But how would you feel if you walked into your room just wanting a relaxing afternoon and your roommate and her boyfriend were there?

Brittany Borstad, junior, Iowa State University, Ames

When my roommate started dating his present girlfriend, she was in our room constantly. Don't get me wrong; she was nice, but I have problems falling asleep when two people are nose to nose, whispering to each other in the bed six feet from me in a direct line of sight.

Justin Brookens, freshman, Drake University, Des Moines, IA

GET THIS! THREE BEST "KEEP OUT" SIGNALS

1. A favorite quote—probably closer to Willy Wonka than William Shakespeare—on the whiteboard outside your room.
2. Roll of masking tape or a scrunchy on the doorknob.
3. A text message to your roommate that the room is on fire, so be a good citizen and stay out of the way.

> ### DID WE MENTION THAT . . .
>
> ▶ One student said the keep-out signal he and his roommate used
> was "Hey, can you get lost for an hour?" But everyone knew
> it, so half the floor ended up outside his room singing, "Let's
> Get It On."

Most of the time, a girl who is going to shack will stay at the frat house.
Joanna Stone, senior, University of Mississippi, Oxford

My friend's roommate would come back drunk, with a girl. And my
friend would wake up in the middle of the night and there they'd be.
It was awkward.
Brian Steimers, junior, University of Delaware, Newark

Her boyfriend was over at our place a lot. She realized it was kinda
getting to bug me. We changed some things so he wouldn't stay
nights before I had a big test and they wouldn't use my stuff without
asking. We were respectful so we didn't have big problems, and we
either talked it through or I sometimes left the room to have some
breathing space.
Jessica Monroe, sophomore, Butler University, Indianapolis

It's rude to have sex while your roommate is there. Just sleeping over
is different.
Rachel Lenz, junior, Vassar College, Poughkeepsie, NY

Chapter 6

An Rx for Roommate/ Residence Hall Hassles

Until you live 24/7 with 59 other people, you really can't imagine what it's like. And you can't ease into it an hour at a time. Rather, you move in, gasp at the bathrooms, think shower shoes, and, with some adjustments, get on with your life. There'll be long (and sometimes loud) nights and *no* clean clothes, and your food in the communal refrigerator probably will disappear. Tack onto those annoyances the fact that minority issues flare up, valuables go into lockdown, and some parties are legendary. Communal living, one of college's most unique experiences— you'll figure it out and have stories to tell friends back home.

Who Comes in to Clean This Place?

I call Mom and she comes and cleans—happily. I think she misses me. I am truly grateful.

Sandra Lazo de la Vega, sophomore, Florida Atlantic University, Wilkes Honors College, Jupiter

So far, it's been me because I make the most mess.

Alix Lifka-Reselman, freshman, Brandeis University, Waltham, MA

You look under your bed one day, see a whole layer of stuff, and say, "Where did that come from?"

Harrison Macris, sophomore, Boston University

Freshmen are notorious for getting sick because they don't know how to drink. Clean up after yourself. That shouldn't even have to be said.

Sage Middleton, senior, Tulane University, New Orleans

GET THIS! AN R.A.'S TAKE ON COMMUNAL LIVING

Do ...

- Remember that people usually live below and above you.
- Bring headphones. (Loudspeakers are great, but not always appropriate.)
- *Use Febreze.* The stages of clothes are clean, worn, and dirty. Wash if dirty. Rewear if worn. Febreze is key to extending the life of your wardrobe and keeping costs down.
- Stay up really late sometimes. So many people are up at all hours that odds are you'll meet new people and have wonderful conversations with familiar ones.

Don't ...

- Get off on the wrong foot with the people living on either side of you (or your roommate, for that matter)—they can make your life hellacious.
- Leave your kitchenware in the communal kitchen (unless you don't care if everyone else uses it and leaves it dirty).
- Leave your food or drink in the communal refrigerator unless it is packaged and labeled multiple times as yours.

Ryan Scofield, senior, former R.A., College of William and Mary, Williamsburg, VA

I figured because I never used the dishes in the suite kitchen, it wasn't up to me whether they got cleaned or not. Looking back, even if the dishes aren't yours, help clean them for the sake of hygiene and because everything you do doesn't have to be convenient for you.

Alan Kistler, senior, Fordham University, New York

GET THIS! LITTLE LESSONS MAYBE NOBODY TAUGHT YOU—YET

- The fridge is not just a long-term cold-storage box. Be wary of food that's now green but didn't used to be.
- Unless your dorm is next to a meat-packing plant, fresh air through open windows is a good thing.
- No rags or cleaning supplies? Cut up a raggedy T-shirt, smear on a little laundry detergent, and wipe stuff down.
- Resolve gets hair dye and vomit out of the carpet.

I was beyond disappointed when I learned I'd be living in the all-female dorm. But as it turns out, that was the cleanest dorm on campus. The staff that cleaned the hallways and bathrooms appreciated us for not destroying the dorm on the weekends.

Jenn Mulroe, senior, University of Connecticut, Storrs

GET THIS! TOP 10 BEST ON-CAMPUS HOUSING

1. Scripps College, Claremont, CA
2. Loyola College–Maryland, Baltimore, MD
3. George Washington University, Washington, DC
4. Harvey Mudd College, Claremont, CA
5. Harvard University, Cambridge, MA
6. Pepperdine University, Malibu, CA
7. Bryn Mawr College, Bryn Mawr, PA
8. Bowdoin College, Brunswick, ME
9. Rice University, Houston, TX
10. Emerson College, Boston, MA

We had probably the worst thing in the world—six girls to one bathroom. We made up a cleaning schedule, but only three of us followed it. You'd say something to the others and they'd say, "Oh, yeah, I was going to do it later." Sometimes they would, but it wasn't that good a job. Even so, it wasn't worth a fight. You live in such close quarters and don't have your own space anyway. Then, fighting over the bathroom?

Lauren Press, junior, University of Denver

Gross Showers, Who Left the Toilet Seat Up, and Who Peed on the Seat Again?

The bathrooms are nasty. When you're sharing a bathroom with 50 other people, getting sick is going to happen.

Rebecca Zwisler, senior, St. Mary's College, Notre Dame, IN

Bathrooms were a shock. There were four showers for 40 girls. You had a shower curtain and a little changing room with another curtain. You get used to it.

Beth Giudicessi, senior, University of Notre Dame (IN)

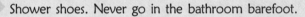

GET THIS! WHAT TO WEAR? WHAT TO WEAR?

▶ Shower shoes. Never go in the bathroom barefoot.

Sage Middleton, senior, Tulane University, New Orleans

A bathrobe so you can change in your room. And don't let your towel touch anything. Get out of the bathroom as fast as you can. I saw how they come in to clean. They wipe down the toilet and sink with the same cloth.

Shakira Ali, sophomore, Loyola University, Chicago

Some guys wore boxers in the halls, but at least they were covered.

Rachel Lenz, junior, Vassar College, Poughkeepsie, NY

I have to change the toilet paper all the time. People won't even put the new roll on the holder.

Anna Skelly, senior, California State University–Long Beach

DID WE MENTION THAT . . .

▶ If there are two pairs of feet in the shower next to you, and one belongs to a him and the other belongs to a her, do you still ask if they have any hot water?

We use the boys' bathroom next door because it's so close to our room. They have no respect. Boys pee on the seats. They cut their hair and leave hair in the sink. The hacking phlegm sounds are awful. We're supposed to bring up concerns at hall meetings. For example, I yelled at the phlegm guy and he just got pissed off.

Alix Lifka-Reselman, freshman, Brandeis University, Waltham, MA

How Hard Can It Be to Do Laundry?

One moment, you can't wait for the freedom and the next, you say, "Oh, my gosh! Who's going to do my laundry?" My mother gave me a book of instructions.

Katie Loberg, junior, Loyola University, Chicago

Everyone said, "You'll never last that far from home" because my mom always did my laundry. I just let it stack up until I have tons and tons to do, like six machines.

Jessica Monroe, sophomore, Butler University, Indianapolis

I learned how to do laundry when I was probably in fourth grade. There are definitely kids here who can't do laundry. Some guys just put Febreze on their clothes.

Cassius Harris, sophomore, Oberlin (OH) College

DID WE MENTION THAT . . .

Clothes that require dry cleaning or special care when washing—turning them inside out, cold water, delicate cycle—might cause more hassle than you want to squeeze into your brand-new life.

DID WE MENTION THAT . . .

▶ One student put off washing her sheets until it was almost literally time to leave for the airport for Thanksgiving vacation. At that last minute, she decided she just couldn't come back to dirty sheets, so she vacuumed them.

If you're going to leave your clothes in the dryer, do laundry at 2 A.M. Otherwise, someone will come along and throw your dry clothes on the floor or in the garbage so they can use the dryer.

Shakira Ali, sophomore, Loyola University, Chicago

Save your quarters. Also, if you put a dollar bill in a vending machine and press "coin return," it gives you back four quarters.

Meghan Hannahs, junior, Westminster College, Salt Lake City

GET THIS! WHEN TO DO LAUNDRY

- Never on Sunday, because everybody else is doing it then.
- Same goes for the day before break.
- Even your favorite dirty sweatpants seem dirty.
- When you have a full load. Otherwise, you're wasting money.
- Every time you're home. It's free, and if you're lucky, a parent will take pity on you and fold it.

Be aware of your clutter. I didn't let the laundry on my bed become the laundry on his bed.

Alan Kistler, senior, Fordham University, New York

Nobody wants the stench of your rotting, three-week-old workout clothes consuming the whole hallway.

Ryan Scofield, senior, College of William and Mary, Williamsburg, VA

You don't need an iron. Just hang things up or steam things in the shower.

Raija Bushnell, freshman, DePauw University, Greencastle, IN

GET THIS! ALIX'S TAKE ON LAUNDRY

1. My roommate showed me about separating clothes for different kinds of washing. Separating is overrated.
2. If you don't do your laundry often enough, it starts to take over your room and you have to sit on it. I'm using my laundry as a chair right now.

Alix Lifka-Reselman, freshman, Brandeis University, Waltham, MA

It's Like a Party 24/7

Our neighbors used to blast Avril Lavigne like every day. It got to the point that we could hardly stand it and we'd bang on the walls. I wouldn't really suggest this; I guess it kind of adds tension.

Brenna Derksen, freshman, University of Iowa, Iowa City

If you are not a verbal person, you can write a note or have a third party present for saying your concerns.

Sarah Sentz, sophomore, University of Montana, Missoula

GET THIS! BLESSED HEADPHONES

One student we know had two roommates. The first brought parties back to the dorm, which did not make the religiously conservative roommate happy at all. Those two roommates would get into long, involved, sometimes loud discussions, so our student simply put on headphones.

I live in the more quiet freshman dorm that has its fair share of social life. I wanted my living area to be a place I can go to for calmness and serenity.

Laura Polden, freshman, George Washington University, Washington, DC

My new roommate's ex-roommates were always partying and making noise late at night. Sometimes she slept in my room to be able to make her 8 o'clock classes. They say to work it out with roommate issues, but sometimes you just have to get out.

Olamide Oduyingbo, freshman, Quinnipiac University, Hamden, CT

I was in the quiet study dorm when I first got to school. After a week, I transferred with my roommates to a livelier, upbeat, social dorm. It was a big change for the better.

Anonymous

20/20 HINDSIGHT

I was in an overcrowded, loud, party dorm, and one roommate was a huge partyer. We never fought and I wanted to stick it out, but friends said moving would be better for everybody, that there was no point in sticking it out. At Halloween, Res Life matched me with a girl who had had a similar experience and I moved. If your lifestyle doesn't match your roommates' or the dorm's, it's not necessarily a bad thing to move. My other roommates and I are fine with each other now and people in the new dorm were very accepting.

Emily Cullings, junior, Colgate University, Hamilton, NY

Some students can balance party and work better than others, but every day of the week?

Jason Kaplan, senior, Colgate University, Hamilton, NY

People still up at 3 A.M. are not quiet. Hall hours don't matter.

Brittany Borstad, junior, Iowa State University, Ames

There's a piano in the parlor under my room, with quiet hours for no playing. I've heard someone playing the piano until 2:30 A.M. and it makes my floor vibrate. I e-mailed the hall president (no R.A.s), but nothing changed. Sometimes you are at the mercy of boorish people.

Rachel Lenz, junior, Vassar College, Poughkeepsie, NY

DID WE MENTION THAT . . .

If you are uncomfortable about others' use of alcohol or drugs in your room, suite, or pod but you don't want to rat people out, pull your roommate aside and give him or her a chance to move the party. Say if the party is not gone in 10 minutes that you'll have to call the R.A. or campus police. Of course, then you have to do it, too.

If you are not old enough to drink in your dorm, don't take the chance. Getting caught is twice as bad in the dorm as it is outside of the dorm.

Amie Reed, junior, Illinois State University, Normal

You can jabber with friends, but telling an R.A. about a problem might make something happen. I wish more students would come to me before there's a blowup and the roommates are in a knot that's hard to untangle. If we were working on the problem as we went along, it would be easier for them and me.

Laura MacLean, senior, R.A., University of Notre Dame (IN)

Respect the dorm rules. Not everybody has your agenda.

Harrison Macris, sophomore, Boston University

Where Is Everyone?

We don't have Friday classes, so Thursday night, about two people are left on campus, and there's nothing to do. When I had to spend a weekend on campus, I'd rent movies to watch on this huge TV in our dorm, and get expensive take-out food. I pretended I was rich.

Sandra Lazo de la Vega, sophomore, Florida Atlantic University, Wilkes Honors College, Jupiter

---

You won't get connected to your roommate and people you share a common bond with if you run home more than once a month.

Aimee Ludlow, sophomore, Florida State University, Tallahassee

---

Our campus is 50 percent commuters. It's different to me because I never thought of going to college and living at home. That takes away some of college life and those experiences. But some people need that family connection.

Jessica Monroe, sophomore, Butler University, Indianapolis

I didn't want to go potluck, so I roomed with a girl from my high school. But she went home every weekend. I felt lonely so I started going home, too.

Chelsea Chaney, junior, Washburn University, Topeka, KS

GET THIS! TOP EIGHT REASONS TO STAY AT SCHOOL ON WEEKENDS

1. On Saturday morning, your parent doesn't come into your room all Mary Sunshine and say, "Did you know it's already 9 o'clock? Day's a-wasting."
2. Nobody's going to ask, "How do you like school?"
3. You don't have family errands like carting a month's recycling to bins across town.
4. You plus three other kids in your dorm are enough for 2-on-2 pickup basketball or volunteering to work on a Habitat for Humanity house.
5. Your parents love you. They miss you. But after 18 years, give them a weekend alone!
6. Eventually your high school friends will stay at their school on weekends; then you'll be spending Saturday night renting movies with your crazy aunt and little brother.
7. Your mom can't ask you why you're not drinking milk.
8. You might meet the love of your life ... or the love of the week, which is fine, too.

Minority Issues

[When] the majority is Caucasian, I feel that results in a certain level of discomfort—not regularly being with people who look like you. Try to find people you are comfortable with. If that means looking for other minority students or clubs, that's fine. At the same time, don't be afraid to venture out and talk to other people. You'll be living with them for the next four years, so take advantage and learn about their cultures.

Akwasi Agyemang, sophomore, Boston University

As a minority, sports helped. Being part of a team gives you a sense of family. You meet people of different races, ethnicities, backgrounds, and after two weeks, you feel like you've known them a long time.

Cassius Harris, sophomore, Oberlin (OH) College

GET THIS! HOW SHAKIRA SEES IT

Growing up, I would never let anything get to me. If I was the only minority in a classroom, I would never feel like someone was being rude just because I was a minority. It might have been like that, but I was oblivious to it. If you don't make it an issue for yourself, others won't make it an issue for you. There have been times at college where I have been asked where I am from, and it seems like Texas is not a sufficient answer, which is weird because I don't ask people, "Where are you from? Italy? Ireland?"

Shakira Ali, sophomore, Loyola University, Chicago

We had more freedom to voice our opinions in the classroom—as long as you could back yourself up—because our teacher acted as a moderator in case anything started to get out of hand. But be careful when you're not in the classroom, which is hard when you're not used to being around minority groups. Learn to keep quiet until you know what boundaries you can and cannot cross. For example, I'm a white girl from the country, and one time an African American student did my hair, and I jokingly called it "ghetto" and she was offended. I apologized but things didn't seem the same between us after that.

Amie Reed, junior, Illinois State University, Normal

At the beginning of one class, the teacher was trying to say my name in taking attendance. She said it a couple of times, but still didn't get it right, scribbled something on her roll sheet, and moved on. The next day she didn't call my name. After class I asked if she'd marked me here. She said she knew who I was so she didn't call out my name. But I saw her roll sheet and she'd written down what I looked like. I was a little offended but I really just ignore it. She's the one who's giving me my grade.

Olamide Oduyingbo, freshman, Quinnipiac University, Hamden, CT

For people of different backgrounds, learning to get along is trial-and-error. You make mistakes because you don't understand. As an R.A., I saw more issues with sexuality and culture-clash concerns than with race.

Adam Berry, senior, Emory University, Atlanta

GET THIS! STRAIGHT TALK FROM A LESBIAN STUDENT

- I wish colleges would include a box on the registration form that says, "I'm gay," or "I'm straight," or "I'm willing to live with a gay [roommate]." I know it's intrusive, but it would be so helpful. It got really awkward with my roommate because she didn't know about me.
- If your college has a gay/lesbian or gay/lesbian/straight alliance, attend the first couple of meetings, but don't expect too much. It may be more of a time to socialize than an activist group.
- Don't out yourself right away, because you never know who you'll alienate. If I had told my friends sooner, some wouldn't have stayed.
- If you are really harassed, go to the dean of students. Give names of students. You're not a snitch. You are paying to be at the school.

Lori Donovan, junior, St. Olaf College, Northfield, MN

My roommate and I hit it off right away. On our second day, I asked what we should do if we bring guys over. "Oh, that reminds me," she said, and she showed me a picture of her girlfriend. I've never been really close with a homosexual before, but I went into it completely open-minded. We were like sisters all year, even though we ran around with different groups. This year, we each chose a roommate from the friends in our own groups. But I miss her when I don't see her. College is an open market of ideas, and living with someone with a completely different background gives you insight. She and I joked that we would make a funny sit-com. She's a liberal from the conservative Midwest and I'm a Republican from New York City.

Katia Porzecanski, sophomore, Tufts University, Medford, MA

DID WE MENTION THAT . . .

Making fun of someone's music—whether it's hip-hop, Celtic, or country—may seem like a jab at the person's ethnicity or race, intended or not. One student told us that her music was "almost like part of where I come from."

I definitely experienced culture shock regarding the class difference at Brown. Everyone had . . . stuff. Lots of it. Very expensive, also. I had never experienced such opulence since my parents and I have always led a very simple life. Imagine your peers carrying items you only saw in high-end fashion magazines. It was overwhelming briefly, but I realized those students were still very down-to-earth and interested in their peers. While there is some discomfort at first from class stratification, the students handle the issues pretty well.

Sri Kalyanaraman, junior, Brown University, Providence, RI

Theft and Personal Safety

There are no massive criminals coming into Hamilton, New York. We have those small, blue emergency towers all over, and the last time they were used was probably to find out the score of a Colgate-Cornell hockey game.

Jason Kaplan, senior, Colgate University, Hamilton, NY

Figure out where those little emergency phones are, and program the emergency number into your cell phone.

Christina Hoffman, junior, Harvard University, Cambridge, MA

DID WE MENTION THAT . . .

▶ Here's a surprise: Most campus crimes are committed by students, not sinister strangers from the outside world. And pretty much every campus has some crime. So be aware of the potential for danger. For example, rape is the most violent crime on U.S. campuses; often, date rape drugs are involved. In fact, alcohol and drug abuse is involved in about 90 percent of campus crimes.

Lock anything in your closet you don't want taken.

Jeff Eskew, senior, Texas Christian University, Fort Worth

There's not as much theft when you live up on the third or fourth floor. Still, get in the habit of bringing your room key everywhere.

Christina Hoffman, junior, Harvard University, Cambridge, MA

Lock your laptop to the leg of your desk with a cable lock. One kid came on a Monday and stole a few laptops, then came back the next day, at the same time, wearing the same clothes. I was watching TV and my roommate was on the computer. This kid walks in, freezes up, says, "I'm sorry. I must be in the wrong room." We noticed he had one laptop under his shirt already. He got caught.

Brian Steimers, junior, University of Delaware, Newark

GET THIS! STREET SMARTS 101

• Your best defense against becoming a victim of on-campus crime is common sense. Know your routes on campus and in the neighborhood. Create a network of friends; give their phone numbers to your parents and advisers.

• Take advantage of informative programs, literature, and postings from your campus security office. That office deals with everything from student escort services to emergencies and fire issues, law enforcement and securing buildings, to making sure nobody's in your parking spot.

• Have a designated nondrinking buddy. Walking home late at night isn't very smart; walking home late at night drunk and alone is just plain stupid.

The neighborhood we're in isn't the safest so I wouldn't consider walking alone at night on campus. We usually try to have a guy with a group. Campus security definitely has a presence; it's not hidden in an office somewhere.

Katie Beno, freshman, Gonzaga University, Spokane, WA

Keep the 800-numbers, resource numbers, and other school numbers they give you. I used them several times, like when I needed to call campus security to let me in my room when I locked myself out.

Sarah Sentz, sophomore, University of Montana, Missoula

I feel safe in the dorms and while walking around practically anywhere. I wouldn't say I have street smarts, and I'm probably kind of naive, but I'm still here in one piece—cars haven't run me over ... yet.

Robyn Lee, junior, New York University, New York

GET THIS! TOP 10 BEST SAFETY AND SECURITY

1. Boston College, Chestnut Hill, MA
2. West Point, West Point, NY
3. Wake Forest University, Winston-Salem, NC
4. Dartmouth College, Hanover, NH
5. Bard College, Annandale-on-Hudson, NY
6. Southwestern University, Georgetown, TX
7. Colgate University, Hamilton, NY
8. Bowdoin College, Brunswick, ME
9. Davidson College, Davidson, NC
10. Purdue University, West Lafayette, IN

7

Okay, Time to Study

Here you are meeting lots of people, adjusting to a roommate, hoping Mom will send food, and then you have to study, too. The thing is, you just cannot imagine how hard–and different–the academic life will be. Success now starts with learning how to learn, college-style. Actual thinking replaces busywork, assignments are huge, and the professors don't care if you're hung over or have the flu. There's a trade-off for spending only a few hours a day in class–even no hours some days–and that is managing your time (as opposed to your parents keeping track for you). How (and how much) to study, when, where, and with whom require planning and discipline. You can dig yourself into a hole by October, when climbing out is already difficult at best. And the last phone call you want to make is "Dad, come pick me up. And bring the van."

Hey, This Isn't High School

My first semester I had 19 credits and worked 15 hours a week. The first day, I had all five classes. I cried at the end of the day, thinking I couldn't do it. The next day, I wrote out a weekly calendar for each class and followed it.

Bryn Rouse, sophomore, University of Montana, Missoula

The first day of classes, the syllabi are overwhelming and scary. Within two days you know every assignment you have for the whole semester! I wondered, "Will I be able to get everything done?" Now, if don't get a syllabus, I'm not organized.

Martha Edwards, senior, Marquette University, Milwaukee

DID WE MENTION THAT . . .

> Students keep telling us you absolutely, positively *must* read your syllabi–every word, especially for deadlines!

The difference between high school and college is like a big shock. In high school, maybe you'd put in a couple of hours the night before the test and do fine. I got a D on my first psychology test in college.

Niki Grangruth, senior, St. Olaf College, Northfield, MN

You aren't used to working as hard as you do in college, and you won't have parents on your back saying, "Do your homework!"

Rebecca Zwisler, senior, St. Mary's College, Notre Dame, IN

> ## DID WE MENTION THAT . . .
>
> Once you figure out how to be in charge of yourself, you'll wonder why it took you so long.
> - Create a system that allows you to keep track of everything you need to do every day.
> - Do what's most important first, even if you hate doing it.
> - Pace yourself, work hard, and take breaks. You'll need them.
> - Learn to say no. Being successful is not a popularity contest. Actually, you *can't* do it all.

You get lots of crap and busywork in high school. College assignments actually are pertinent to what you're learning.

Ande Davis, senior, Washburn University, Topeka, KS

> College is not a lot harder than high school. It's just a different way of learning.
>
> *Becca Strutt, senior, Hope College, Holland, MI*

When I first got here, I thought they all were so much smarter, more hardworking. In calculus class I thought everyone was getting it and I'm not. I was scared, but I found out later that everyone else was just as clueless.

Erin Pirruccello, sophomore, University of Pennsylvania, Wharton School, Philadelphia

Homework is not doing workbook sheets but rather reading the whole book.

Zack Barr, freshman, Brandeis University, Waltham, MA

You have a lot more work, but you have a lot more time to do it. You might have 150 pages of reading, but you usually have only three hours of class a day instead of seven like in high school. So you can begin that reading at 1 o'clock.

Caitlin Wells, sophomore, Grinnell (IA) College

It's so easy to run off and enjoy the block of free time. I'm a wanderer and go to see the monuments and other sights and feel good about it. Then here I am working Sunday night on a paper and say, "God, why did I do that?"

Clark Young, freshman, Georgetown University, Washington, DC

20/20 HINDSIGHT

This year I get up and work early in the morning rather than at 1 A.M. No one else is up so you can think better and get done what you need to faster.

Katharine McCormick, sophomore, University of Pennsylvania, Philadelphia

There are no little checks to keep you on track. No homework assignments to turn in every week. No little pop quizzes and exams. It's all about self-motivation.

Henna Messina, senior, Fordham University, New York

They take roll in college, but you can still show up or not. It's up to you.

Jennifer Bowen, sophomore, Westminster College, Salt Lake City

Go to classss!!!!! Even though some classes are "easy" and most classes don't take attendance, the sheer volume of material you miss in a class period is enough to set you far behind!

Katie Ablan, sophomore, Indiana University–Bloomington

Freshman year, I was at class all of the time. Sophomore year, not so much. By junior year, I showed up only for tests. I didn't fail, but I didn't do great, either. I wouldn't recommend this method, but missing one or two classes won't kill you.

Anonymous

GET THIS! FIVE TIPS FOR STUDENTS WITH DISABILITIES

If you have physical or learning disabilities, you may need to:

- take the initiative even before the first week and say, "I need help." Until then, no one is watching out to make sure you are getting your prescribed accommodations. Even if you don't want accommodations, go meet the director of the LD program;
- realize that not everyone knows about appropriate and legal accommodations. If there's a problem, go to the director of the LD program or another administrator;
- consider lightening your class load to the minimum credits needed to be a full-time student, even if it takes longer to graduate. Many students take five years or longer to graduate;
- use the university's writing center to help with papers; hire tutors if they aren't provided;
- join an activity that does things that are fun and meaningful to you.

Usually, carrying a computer around is not allowed in high school, so computers were something that only existed for some assignments at home. But here, people take them to the library, classes, the coffee shop—everywhere.

Nathan Pflueger, freshman, Stanford (CA) University

When all the lecture notes are online, it's easier if you miss a formula or some notes. But it doesn't replace going to class and talking to the professor and hearing an explanation.

Laura MacLean, senior, University of Notre Dame (IN)

> I take virtually no notes in class because usually the lecture coincides with the book. So I prop open the book and put Post-it notes where the teacher is lecturing.
>
> *Fadi Bayaa, junior, California State University–Long Beach*

There aren't as many grades going into the grade book, so projects and assignments account for a bigger percentage of your overall grade.

Rachel Pfennig, freshman, DePauw University, Greencastle, IN

Go out on a limb. In a given class, 20 out of 25 students will make the same hackneyed arguments in their papers. The five students who put forth something a bit more original will get the A's. Always attempt to develop a novel argument—even if you are afraid your prof might disagree with it—because your prof (unless he likes conformity) will respect your audacity and independent-thinking ability.

Sean Harris, junior, Harvard University, Cambridge, MA

GET THIS! THREE WAYS COLLEGE PAPERS DIFFER FROM HIGH SCHOOL PAPERS

1. Professors don't precisely answer your question, "What do you want in this paper?" Instead, they talk about what makes a well-researched and well-written paper without telling you specifically how to get there.
2. Rather than a summary of a dazzling array of sources, professors expect analysis leading to an original or thoughtful conclusion. You always had to present the "what." Now you must present the "why."
3. Extensions? Hardly ever. Plan that the final deadline is your *only* deadline.

If a teacher says you can hand in a paper late, keep that e-mail, because the teacher may forget what was said. They do a lot more than just teach your class.

Elizabeth Pitruzzello, senior, Central Connecticut State University, New Britain

High school is so social. In college, you're with people who have a strong work ethic like yours. Everything you talk about is either boys or studying.

Jacqueline Cuisinier, senior, St. Mary's College, Notre Dame, IN

Studying is one thing I could have done a whole lot more of freshman year. I think I was still coming off a minor senior high school slump and didn't have the discipline or drive I needed to deal with five college courses.

Andrew Balkam, senior, Georgetown University, Washington, DC

Even if your school has a lot of academic resources, you're still really on your own and must manage your time. It's hard. I took a course on learning skills, including how to take notes.

Cassius Harris, sophomore, Oberlin (OH) College

My first year I averaged three to four hours of classes per day versus my more than eight-hour days in high school. The result was way more free time than I knew what to do with. However, the time I *did* dedicate to homework was less productive, partly because of having a roommate, random visitors, and my computer right next to me. So while I had more free time, I spent more of it working to achieve the GPA I wanted.

David Neumann, sophomore, University of Southern California, Los Angeles

Professors—Pretty Important People

I had trouble deciding what level of Japanese classes to take, so I got the Japanese teacher's phone number on the school Web site and called her (during the summer before freshman year). We ended up talking for an hour. It was cool because when I came to school, she already knew me. Now, she is my academic adviser.

Emily Cullings, junior, Colgate University, Hamilton, NY

I had to miss a few weeks of school before finals because my dad was sick. I thought I was screwed. I e-mailed the professors and all five set aside time with me. Like I met with my calc professor four hours every day, the week before the exam.

Katia Porzecanski, sophomore, Tufts University, Medford, MA

20/20 HINDSIGHT

As a freshman, I took lots of classes with more than 100 students and I thought the professors wouldn't remember me. One day the T.A. in my discussion section said, "The professor has said he really respects how you pay attention in lecture." I should have gone to see that professor to get to know him to get advice when I needed it.

Kendra Boeckman, senior, Oklahoma State University, Stillwater

Even if you understand the material, even if you don't have a question, ask one anyway. Just so the teacher can know who you are.

Shakira Ali, sophomore, Loyola University, Chicago

GET THIS! TOP 10 COLLEGES WITH THE BEST ACADEMIC ATMOSPHERE

1. Princeton University, Princeton, NJ
2. MIT, Cambridge, MA
3. Williams College, Williamstown, MA
4. Stanford University, Stanford, CA
5. Georgetown University, Washington, DC
6. Seattle University, Seattle, WA
7. Swarthmore College, Swarthmore, PA
8. Yale University, New Haven, CT
9. Harvey Mudd College, Claremont, CA
10. University of Chicago, Chicago, IL

DID WE MENTION THAT . . .

> You don't necessarily have to be cleaning a professor's office to get an A. But going in for help or to talk about things in class or outside of school isn't going to get an A, either.

Professors hate it when students want to know if they're getting a B+ or an A-. They want students to pursue excellence for the sake of learning.

Graham Shepherd, senior, DePauw University, Greencastle, IN

Note professors and T.A.s you do and do not like as teachers. Some professors are worse teachers than T.A.s. Take another class from teachers you like just for fun or because you are interested in the topic.

Bryn Rouse, sophomore, University of Montana, Missoula

20/20 HINDSIGHT

I was working toward a degree in sports management, taking the required classes and meeting the minimum GPA requirements. When I applied to that school (as a college senior), I was told the (minimum) GPA had gone up significantly and I did not qualify. I ended up with probably 75 hours of credit that meant nothing. It wasn't KU's fault. I'd only seen my adviser at the beginning of freshman year and again at the beginning of senior year. A huge school can't give individual attention. You cannot wait for teachers and advisers to baby you. You have to make things happen yourself.

John Schmidt, senior, University of Kansas, Lawrence

You are paying for the teachers to help you. During sophomore year, I couldn't get the hang of a required computer programming class. I vowed to go to my teacher every day if I had to, and I ended up doing pretty well because of it.

Amie Reed, junior, Illinois State University, Normal

See professors on their time. Don't be afraid to spend 30 minutes discussing a point you're having problems with. Most professors are happy to have somebody knock on the door.

Jesse Herwitz, junior, Fordham University, New York

GET THIS! RATING THE PROFESSOR

Want to know what other students think about your professors? Want to let other students know what you think? Go to www.ratemyprofessors.com, where students rate professors on Easiness, Clarity, Helpfulness, and Hotness. Yeah, that's right. Hotness.

Or, if you have a MySpace.com account, try out the "Grade My Professor" option that lets students leave letter grades and comments for Lectures, Homework, Tests, Fairness, Grading, and Accessibility.

Before I choose classes, I definitely use ratemyprofessors.com.

Brian Steimers, junior, University of Delaware, Newark

I have gone to ratemyprofessors.com but, that can be skewed, so I'd rather ask people I trust for their opinion.

Katie Beno, freshman, Gonzaga University, Spokane, WA

Love/Hate 8 A.M. Classes

Nobody likes them.

Caitlin Wells, sophomore, Grinnell (IA) College

Odds are that sometimes you'll just be going to bed by then.

Ryan Scofield, senior, College of William and Mary, Williamsburg, VA

In afternoon classes, it's tough to focus. You just had lunch, the sun's out, and it's a perfect time not to be stuck in class.

Fadi Bayaa, junior, California State University–Long Beach

If you have to get out of bed for 8 o'clock classes, I say get a bunch of good-natured teachers.

Jennifer Bowen, sophomore, Westminster College, Salt Lake City

It was brutal just staying awake. In high school you go to bed at 10, but in college, it's 2 or 3 A.M. Coffee becomes a lifesaver.

Graham Shepherd, senior, DePauw University, Greencastle, IN

> ## DID WE MENTION THAT . . .
>
> ▶ You rarely get shut out of an 8 o'clock—or even 8:30 A.M.—class. And you can wear pajamas.

If you take an early class, make sure it's one you're interested in. I went the first two weeks, every day. After that, I went the day before a test, the day of the test, and the day after. I pulled a B because I'm a lucky multiple-choice student.

Ande Davis, senior, Washburn University, Topeka, KS

I decided I wasn't going to be anybody's mom in college. If somebody can't make it in college, how are they going to make it in the real world? You should not be expected to wake up your roommate so he can get to class.

Paul Bromen, junior, St. Olaf College, Northfield, MN

Try to get Fridays off from classes, too (along with no 8 o'clocks).

Abby Beaves, freshman, St. Cloud (MN) State University

GET THIS! HOW TO GET UP FOR 8 O'CLOCKS

- Do not put your alarm clock right by your bed or you'll hit snooze and go back to sleep. Until noon.
- When the choice is between sleeping 20 more minutes or taking a shower, you *should* take a shower, but you'll probably sleep.
- Promise yourself an afternoon nap. Maybe even two afternoon naps.
- Consider only 8 A.M. classes that are less than 10 minutes away from your bed.

Best Study Tips

If the teacher drones and it's a big room, I realize I'm doodling or working a Sudoku puzzle and then class is over and I missed the concept. Also, make sure you are not tired when you go to class, because you won't get it.
Zack Barr, freshman, Brandeis University, Waltham, MA

High school history is facts, dates, people, places. Professors have PhDs in the field and they don't want the chronology of the French Revolution. They want to know how it impacted the rest of Europe. Listen to your professor's take in the lecture and formulate these ideas all semester.
Henna Messina, senior, Fordham University, New York

Do your work in the time you have between classes because you might not want to work every night or you might want to take advantage of things going on at night. This isn't like high school, where you went out only on weekends.
Katia Porzecanski, sophomore, Tufts University, Medford, MA

GET THIS! A HIGH-LEVEL STRATEGY

Jesse Herwitz, junior, Fordham University, New York, suggests the following:

- Study in a way that helps *you* interpret the material. I'm taking Italian, and I don't necessarily go back to the text to study. I might listen to music, watch a movie in Italian, or go online and chat in Italian. That approach is fluid, always moving.

- Create a timeline that gives a mental image of how something happened historically. For a lyrical opera class, I marked each year and date that a piece came out to show the progression and put changes in context.

If studying on your own doesn't work, connect with study groups. I'll keep an appointment with someone to study, but not necessarily with myself. In some classes, people will send an e-mail suggesting anyone interested meet at such-and-such a place and time to study.

Graham Shepherd, senior, DePauw University, Greencastle, IN

Networking is the one thing I learned the most through school. I'd make sure I knew somebody in every class. Then, if you miss or skip a class, get notes from that person and they can get notes from you.

John Schmidt, senior, University of Kansas, Lawrence

Here's the secret it took me a semester to recognize: Most professors do not expect you to carefully do all the reading. Learn how to scan while focusing and actually reading parts that seem important.

R. Matthew Greenawalt, senior, Williams College, Williamstown, MA

GET THIS! FOR THAT EXTRA EDGE

- Use flash cards.
- Highlight, underline, and make margin notes in your textbooks during lecture.
- Take a study break and play a game on your computer. A game. Not games. That means a 10-minute limit.
- Create a study schedule on your PDA, calendar, and cell phone.
- Check out Web sites listed in your textbooks for extra notes, PowerPoints, exams, and chapter summaries—even if the teachers don't refer to them.

You do not have to read all 100 pages that were assigned on the Battle of Blenheim. But, unless your professor is a Churchill enthusiast (in which case, you need to have all 100 pages read and memorized), you need to have at least half of them skimmed.

Sean Harris, junior, Harvard University, Cambridge, MA

Freshmen want to explore everything, talk to everyone, go to all the parties because, God forbid, you don't want to miss one cool thing. Some forget they're also taking classes. So one night a week, don't party. I did that, and even then, I needed more than one night to get all my studying done.

Alan Kistler, senior, Fordham University, New York

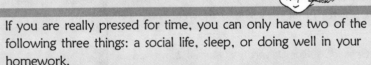

20/20 HINDSIGHT

If you are really pressed for time, you can only have two of the following three things: a social life, sleep, or doing well in your homework.

Marie Giron, freshman, California Institute of Technology, Pasadena

Best Study Hideouts

- The library—although if half the people there are sleeping and the other half are yawning, it might be tough.

- Coffee shops. Take a break and people-watch out the front window.

- A little room at the back of a building. But can you keep it a secret?

- An empty classroom where you can study all night, listening to your iPod and waving at the security guards.

- The classroom where you'll take the test. A picture on a bulletin board you noticed while studying may jog your memory during the test.

- At the beach—depending on the season and your self-discipline.

- On the commuter train.

GET THIS! WHY STUDENTS *DON'T* STUDY IN THEIR ROOMS

- If there's a TV, they'll channel-surf; if not, they'll surf the Web.
- They'll call someone. Anyone, actually.
- They'll start reading a magazine, the label on a bottle of shampoo, their own palm—anything but their required reading.
- They'll be compelled to join a party in progress. Or start one of their own.
- They'll fall asleep.

Testing, Testing

You think you've studied the material for your first college test. But probably you don't really know how to study, which is to study as you go. You can't just study five chapters the night before.

Niki Grangruth, senior, St. Olaf College, Northfield, MN

DID WE MENTION THAT . . .

▶ Being late to the test won't help your stress level.

During finals, I was really freaking out and spent about 15 hours a day studying. I realized this was a bit excessive and decided I needed a break. It was about 2 A.M., but a friend and I decided to go rollerblading and ended up wading in the fountain on campus. I wouldn't have been able to get through finals if I hadn't let loose a little bit.

Molly Harris, sophomore, University of Northern Iowa, Cedar Falls

---

GET THIS! STUDY GROUP TEST PREP TIPS

- Meet with friends, because everyone cares about everyone else's grades.
- Toss around questions like, "How does this work?" and "How does that apply?"
- Identify questions for the professor, and discuss the professor's responses later.
- Spend the last hour or two before the test studying alone.
- Take quick notes to review in case of last-minute questions or blank spots just before the test starts.

Akwasi Agyemang, sophomore, Boston University

DID WE MENTION THAT . . .

One student who stayed up for four days met a friend as she was walking out of her last final. When the friend asked what test she'd just taken, our student couldn't remember. Although we don't recommend this method, the student is on track to graduate in four years.

One finals week, I went from Monday to Thursday without sleep. I could have gone to bed Wednesday night, but I was afraid I wouldn't wake up for my Thursday test. Actually, everyone is going crazy and eating at a 24-hour Steak 'n Shake.

Jacqueline Cuisinier, senior, St. Mary's College, Notre Dame, IN

GET THIS! KISS (KEEP IT SIMPLE, STUDENT)

- It's better to know fewer things really well than to know a lot of things not so well.
- If you just read and don't get it, that's bad.
- Use keywords. If you need to know six things about a topic, have six keywords.
- You probably never will be as prepared as you want to be, so tell yourself you're going to do the best you can and it's going to be okay.
- If you study on your bed, you'll probably fall asleep and wake up with papers all over and crease marks on your face.

It's better to go sick to an exam than to miss it, even if you are coughing and hacking. Make-up tests are really difficult because professors don't want anyone to cheat. Same is true for finals. Professors are supposed to make arrangements if you have more than two exams on one day. But take all the exams as scheduled; it will be easier than taking the harder make-up exam.

Elizabeth Pitruzzello, senior, Central Connecticut State University, New Britain

BELIEVE IT! STREAKER INTERRUPTS TEST

When we were getting ready to take a test in meteorology, this guy comes in, announces he's El Niño, takes off his trench coat, and streaks through the room. The graduate assistant drops the tests, chases him outside—it's winter—and returns carrying the trench coat. Then on the board he writes the license plate number of the car the streaker jumped into. I thought, if my mom only knew what her college education money was going for!

Annon Woodin, senior, Iowa State University, Ames

GET THIS! EXCUSES YOUR PROFESSORS KNOW BY HEART

▶
- My printer broke.
- My computer crashed.
- I wasn't in class so I didn't know ...
- I couldn't get to class because of the (a) blizzard, (b) lightning, (c) heat wave, (d) hangover.
- My grandmother died. (Again.)
- Sob. Sob. Cry. Cry.
- I'm sorry. I have no excuse for this paper being late. (Hey, the truth might just work!)

If you have a disability—I'm a Type 1 diabetic—tell your professors if the disability may affect your academic experience. There may be a test day when my blood sugar is not okay and I am not able to take that test. My professors know I'm not pulling out the diabetes card to get out of this test.

Katie Loberg, junior, Loyola University, Chicago

▶ At test time, lots of my friends lose nine pounds of hair because of the stress. But nothing is that important.

Fadi Bayaa, junior, California State University–Long Beach

Learning to Love Deadlines—or at Least Pay Attention to Them

You hear how important it will be to budget your time, but it's hard to realize what that means until you get in college.

Rachel Pfennig, freshman, DePauw University, Greencastle, IN

It's when people get behind in their schoolwork that they crash and can't handle the pressure anymore.

Chris Petz, senior, University of Washington, Seattle

Panicking is the absolute worst thing you can do. If you start worrying about papers due, you'll not get them done.

Leor Benyamini, junior, Quinnipiac University, Hamden, CT

DID WE MENTION THAT . . .

We Googled "research papers" and within 0.25 seconds had a mind-boggling 9.9 million possibilities. That's handy, but if you copy a line, a paragraph, or a whole paper from online resources or real books and pass the work off as yours, it's plagiarism. Realize that professors also use online resources (among others) to identify copied work. If you're caught, you may earn a failing grade, get kicked out of class, even kicked out of school.

If someone asks you to go out to the movies and you're in the middle of writing a paper, say, "Maybe later." Except when "later" comes, your friends won't go because they waited until the last minute and now they have to write their papers!

Cristina Baptista, graduate student, Fordham University, Bronx, NY

I wait to the last minute because the stress of a deadline works better for me.

Konrad Waliszewski, sophomore, American University, Washington, DC

GET THIS! THAT "P" WORD

If you're a big procrastinator, *deadline* can be a four-letter word.

Ande Davis, senior, Washburn University, Topeka, KS

My definition of procrastination is to go to sleep, make myself wake up at 5 or 6 in the morning, and write the paper that's due that day.

Shakira Ali, sophomore, Loyola University, Chicago

Try my reward system: When you're researching or writing, take a 10-minute break to do whatever you want. Eat a chocolate bar or play a short computer game. Go outside—even if it's cold; breathe deep; get some sun on your face.

Jennifer Bowen, sophomore, Westminster College, Salt Lake City

---

Work ahead when you know you will have a time crunch. When I have a paper, I can't be nervous about getting other things done because I will use that as an excuse to put off doing the paper. It's kind of strange using other work as an excuse.

Katharine McCormick, sophomore, University of Pennsylvania, Philadelphia

If you have a paper due on Friday, you should have a rough draft finished by Sunday evening, so stop by your professor's office during the week to discuss content and style. Such visits allow you to learn what your professor wants the easy way. The hard way, of course, would be receiving low marks on your first few assignments.

Sean Harris, junior, Harvard University, Cambridge, MA

GET THIS! FOUR WAYS TO CLIMB OUT OF A NOSEDIVE

1. Scan your schedule every Sunday night for the upcoming week and even the following week to make sure there aren't any nasty little surprises.
2. List what you must do, prioritize, and figure out what you can let slide if you have a decent grade in that class.
3. Ask for help from your professor and students who get it. It's way too late for fear, shame, or pride.
4. If you are sick, but not yet dying, get up and go to class.

If you want to get A's, you must study more and not procrastinate. If you procrastinate and get a B, you can always tell yourself that you could have gotten an A if you had not procrastinated or if you'd worked harder. I vowed to start my papers early. It's still a theory.

Caitlin Wells, sophomore, Grinnell (IA) College

I'm better now because I finally got sick of being stressed out and being up late.

Amanda Vazzano, senior, Miami University, Oxford, OH

When Too Stressed = Depressed, Get Help

I've learned to manage stress and how it can affect my body and my health. Stress is an evil thing, and there are professionals willing to help by listening or giving you strategies to manage your stress. When you get to college, you may realize that the way you used to handle stress may not give you the same results anymore.

Sara Kaminski, senior, Purdue University, West Lafayette, IN

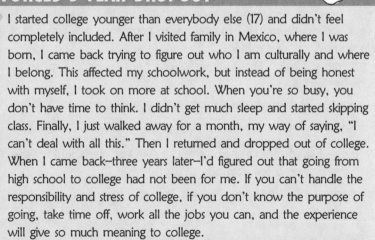

BELIEVE IT! STUDENT'S STRESS FORCES 3-YEAR DROPOUT

I started college younger than everybody else (17) and didn't feel completely included. After I visited family in Mexico, where I was born, I came back trying to figure out who I am culturally and where I belong. This affected my schoolwork, but instead of being honest with myself, I took on more at school. When you're so busy, you don't have time to think. I didn't get much sleep and started skipping class. Finally, I just walked away for a month, my way of saying, "I can't deal with all this." Then I returned and dropped out of college. When I came back—three years later—I'd figured out that going from high school to college had not been for me. If you can't handle the responsibility and stress of college, if you don't know the purpose of going, take time off, work all the jobs you can, and the experience will give so much meaning to college.

Jose Lopez, senior, University of Arkansas, Fayetteville

GET THIS! SIGNS OF DEPRESSION

▶ Being a college student isn't always rah rah I love this place and I'm so happy that I have three exams next week and my relationship isn't going well. Go ahead and feel blue. But realize that some professional help may be needed if you are feeling particularly down, not sleeping well, eating too much or not enough—and all this is lasting longer than two weeks.

If your roommate has signs of depression, you feel bad for the roommate, but the R.A.s should pick up on that. Emotionally, mentally, or physically, as a freshman you aren't able to deal with such roommate issues.

Paul Bromen, junior, St. Olaf College, Northfield, MN

If your roommate has real mental health problems, don't say, "Let me help you with your problems." You aren't a therapist. And don't suggest she get help. That will just offend her. She should go to a counselor herself.

Rebecca Zwisler, senior, St. Mary's College, Notre Dame, IN

If you need psychological help, get it. It's always available for you. You don't even have to tell anybody.

Amie Reed, junior, Illinois State University, Normal

GET THIS! SUICIDE HEADS-UP

Schools want you to be aware of what to do if you feel so down you think about committing suicide. The signs are not always written on a person's forehead, but according to the American Association of Suicidology, they include the following:

- hopelessness
- no reason for living
- rage or uncontrolled anger
- acting recklessly, seemingly without thinking
- feeling like there's no way out
- increased alcohol or drug use
- withdrawing from friends, family, and society
- anxiety
- unable to sleep or sleeping all the time
- dramatic mood changes

If this is you or your roommate, go to the R.A. and/or the counseling or health center for professional help.

Chapter **8**

Really? Free Time!

With a nod to Dr. Seuss—oh, the places you can go and the things you can do when you aren't in class: activities, volunteer opportunities, sports, the Greek system, jobs. This is where you find your niche, meet like-minded students, expand horizons, and have fun. So how can you go wrong? By signing up for everything—or not signing up for anything. The former means an overcommitted you, tied up in knots by fall break. The latter is a one-dimensional you, sick to death of being *only* a student without a life. Try familiar things and new things, stick with what you like, and say, "Thanks, anyway" to the rest. Quitting actually is an honorable option. One caveat for former high school athletes: No matter the division, your commitment will be way more than you ever expected.

Activities and the Pursuit of Happiness

Raija Bushnell, freshman, DePauw University, Greencastle, IN, signed up for the American Cancer Society's Relay for Life and ended up as co-chair for the ceremony: "It's cool to be a freshman in a position of power."

Scott Beggs, senior, Baylor University, Waco, TX, liked what he saw in the student government offices and ran for the student congress: "In high school, you plan proms; in college, you might meet with the school president to discuss why a tuition increase would not benefit the student body."

Ryan Scofield, senior, College of William & Mary, Williamsburg, VA, figured out how to get into student government. "Since class elections were so early freshman year, rather than run for class president against 16 other people, I ran for class secretary to get my foot in the door." (It worked; now Ryan's Student Assembly president.)

Andrew Balkam, senior, Georgetown University, Washington, DC, signed over most of his time second semester to student theater. "I started by working on one production as a carpenter. If you don't run from theater at first, you're sucked into it and tend to spend many of your weekends doing theater stuff."

Katie Jozwik, junior, Columbia College, Chicago, IL, recommends, "Do something different than your major." She switched from being a criminal justice major to mass communication after joining the campus radio station.

Olamide Oduyingbo, freshman, Quinnipiac University, Hamden, CT, joined the Black Students Union to meet friends. "We focus on ways to bring ourselves as one (rather than as separate individuals) into the community and make the community aware there are still minority issues."

Jason Chen, junior, Vassar College, Poughkeepsie, NY, started in his freshman year revitalizing the Vassar Pagan Circle, a group that now receives institutional funding and works to celebrate, explore, and spread awareness about paganism. "If nothing else, I found that leading a group is time consuming. I had to drop a few things, but it has been one of my most rewarding experiences here."

Enough Activities to Fill a Wall Calendar

Get involved right away. Instead of feeling like you've left home and have to be in this strange place until next time you go home, college will become familiar. Then, you'll feel like you have two homes.

Leverett Woodruff, sophomore, Westminster College, Salt Lake City

You learn your interests by trial and error. [The activity you choose] may be related to your discipline or future career, or connect with you culturally or religiously. Actually, finding your interests can be a lifelong process.

Elizabeth Joyce, sophomore, Stanford (CA) University

GET THIS! WARM BODIES

Never heard of broomball? Never learned lines for a school play? No matter. Organizations are looking for warm bodies willing to try something new.

If your passion is underwater badminton and no club exists, create one.

Jason Kaplan, senior, Colgate University, Hamilton, NY

I joined a club through church. It was more like a sorority but no drinking. We do fun exchanges with the boys' club, but without problems like date rape.

Jennifer Bowen, sophomore, Westminster College, Salt Lake City

GET THIS! WHERE'S MY GROUP?

1. Google your school's Web site; pick up information from the activity tables at orientation; read posters on bulletin boards, bathroom doors, and light poles.
2. Ask people in your hall for a thumbs-up or thumbs-down and why.
3. Quiz your R.A., who should know just about everything—or knows somebody who does.
4. Consider any organization that promises food at meetings.
5. Don't join just because you feel pressured to. Actually, especially if you feel pressured.
6. Any group that asks you not to tell anyone about it or the meetings and then asks you for money—probably not a great idea.
7. Do not join a group just because you have a secret crush on someone in the group. If your secret crush asks you to join, well, that's a different story.
8. Once you join, don't miss the meeting where they elect officers or you'll be the new vice president.
9. Don't get a tattoo with the group's logo on it. Seriously.

This is a public school, very liberal, and I wasn't tuned in to how active the Catholic Campus Center is, so I'd just go to Mass on Sunday. But it's always filled with students. I got involved with classes and the tons of social activities, and now my friends and I hang out there.

Katy Cortese, freshman, University of Kansas, Lawrence

If you have a hobby before college, for example, music or sports, keep that up. I'm not a music major, but playing in the school concert band is a great release from my everyday reading/studies (and an easy A).

Chris Petz, senior, University of Washington, Seattle

Being a member of a club maybe takes an hour a week. You won't get paid for the work you do, but it shows you are passionate, motivated to do something, and can take the initiative. It's never negative on the future.

Katie Loberg, junior, Loyola University, Chicago

If you find out an organization really sucks, don't be afraid to quit because you think you'll totally lose out on something. I was on hall counsel because I thought we'd do campuswide events. But all they wanted was for us to plan corridor events. So I quit.

Paul Bromen, junior, St. Olaf College, Northfield, MN

20/20 HINDSIGHT

It's a fairly big adjustment learning to plan activities and prioritize. I found out I have to be very structured with myself. If I tell myself, "I'll do it sometime tonight," it won't work. When I tell myself, "Okay, I'm going to work on this right now until it's done," I don't get distracted and wander off to do something else.

Ian Young, sophomore, Grinnell (IA) College

"I'll Do It! I'll Do It!" Why Volunteering Is a Big Deal

In college, you spend a lot of time thinking more about yourself than others. Volunteering gets you thinking about others, too.

Annon Woodin, senior, Iowa State University, Ames

In FSU's Service Scholar Program, I was required to volunteer for two group projects a semester, maintain a certain GPA, volunteer 75 hours of community service per semester, and attend monthly meetings. The program made freshman year doable and life enjoyable on a humongous campus where it's easy to feel like you are being consumed.

Aimee Ludlow, sophomore, Florida State University, Tallahassee

GET THIS! VOLUNTEER IN YOUR PAJAMAS!

We have an assisted-living home on campus. I just helped plan their senior prom, and I go over for cleaning days and to visit. It makes you feel amazing, you don't get paid, and you can just wear pajamas. It's like, I can't be near my grandparents here, but I have established relationships with these people. If my grandparents are ever in some home like that, I hope someone could come in and listen or pretend to listen to Poppy talk on and on.

Laura Polden, freshman, George Washington University, Washington, DC

You don't see little kids very often when you're in college, so you could volunteer in a mentoring program at a nearby school.

Rachel Pfennig, freshman, DePauw University, Greencastle, IN

Once you start something, it's really bad to quit. I don't need a kid saying, "What happened to my tutor?" I didn't know if I could juggle volunteering and college, so I haven't volunteered in college.

Shakira Ali, sophomore, Loyola University, Chicago

GET THIS! BRIANNA'S BEST REASONS TO GET OFF YOUR DUFF

I wasn't living on the streets growing up, but I did get clothes at the Salvation Army. So my motivation is a little more personal. When I was a freshman, I was asked to help start a campus Rotaract Club. I didn't even know what Rotary was. This spring, I went with Rotary to Xicotepec, Mexico, to plant trees at a school and replace water basins lined with asbestos. Think about volunteering because:

- you may not have a lot of money but you have a healthy body and can work;
- you'll make good friends, even in other countries;
- you'll establish business connections for the future; and
- nothing is more gratifying than the look on the faces of the people you're helping.

Brianna Orton, senior, Drake University, Des Moines, IA

The thing that turns me off is when an activity is poorly managed. With volunteer organizations, you attract people who want to do good, but also people who aren't very good at organization.

James Langlois, junior, Tulane University, New Orleans

GET THIS! VIRTUAL VOLUNTEERING

Call it online volunteering, cyber service, online mentoring, or teletutoring (and that's just for starters)—there are bucketloads of volunteer tasks that can be accomplished via the Internet. Do a Web search and enough sites will pop up to keep you busy until you're 104.

- Correspond with someone who's homebound or in a nursing home.
- Do research for volunteer organizations.
- Build Web sites for nonprofits.

Many organizations require a face-to-face orientation, even for off-site assignments. So if you're a student at Kenyon College in Gambier, OH, don't volunteer for an organization that's across the street from Harvey Mudd College in Claremont, CA.

That Thing About Overcommitment

Starting college and joining 10 clubs is way too much to handle.

Tiffany Wood, junior, Westminster College, Salt Lake City

You want to be involved in everything, but if this is the case, you will wear down and have senioritis by the time you are a sophomore.

Alissa Busha, senior, University of Central Oklahoma, Oklahoma City

GET THIS! IT'S TIME FOR A CHANGE WHEN . . .

1. You take five classes, work 15+ hours a week—then get run down, sick, miss class, and wonder why.
2. You'd be making another to-do list in the shower if only you had a waterproof pen.
3. You're designing the homecoming float on your computer during a physics class lecture.
4. You complain rather than talk about how much you love what you are doing.
5. Your friends don't call before they go out to dinner because they know you're busy.
6. Your parents whine that you never, ever call—and it's true.

Once you say the word in college that you want to get involved, it's all downhill. If you do too much and you don't have time to study at night, it's time to say no.

Chelsea Chaney, junior, Washburn University, Topeka, KS

Finally, I realized I couldn't do everything. If some organizations have something you can do once or twice and you're done, that would be a good bet. And if you are really stressed, don't get in a position where you have a lot of responsibility.

Rachel Pfennig, freshman, DePauw University, Greencastle, IN

GET THIS! MAGIC WORDS TO STAY SANE

- When someone has a fantastic idea for a project, but that someone doesn't have time to actually work on the project, you say, "I don't have time, either."
- When someone asks you to join yet another organization, you say, "No, I'm busy enough."
- When you're pulled every which way but loose, you say, "Sorry, I got overcommitted." It's really as easy to get out as it is to get in.

A Wake-up Call for the Former High School Athlete

I played basketball freshman year at another college. In college the game's four states away, so you travel eight hours, stay in a hotel, do game-day stuff, play the game, travel back, and miss classes. One game can take the whole weekend. When you are on the bus, in the hotel with your friends, it's hard to be disciplined to get good grades.

Konrad Waliszewski, sophomore, American University, Washington, DC

I'd come home from a (varsity) basketball game too tired to work. I finally had to drop a lab because I was tired of asking for extensions, and there was really no way I could make the labs up anyway.

Marie Giron, freshman, California Institute of Technology, Pasadena

DID WE MENTION THAT . . .

One college athlete puts his advice in these terms:
1. Keep your mouth shut. As a new player on the team, spend your time listening and figuring out how things work. Let the coaches do the coaching, and listen to your upperclassmen.
2. Don't brag about how good you were in high school. Nobody cares. College is a whole new level of play, and you need to focus on adapting to it.

Even though I was a varsity tennis player in high school, I knew it would take up all my time in college. I wanted to be in a sorority, handle an internship, and academics. Sports weren't at the top of my priorities anymore. If you still want to be an athlete and still have that competitive spirit, do intramurals.

Katie Loberg, junior, Loyola University, Chicago

Look in the mirror and ask yourself: "Am I willing to dedicate myself wholly to this sport?" You can't say, "I'm going to do this because it's fun." The rowing team gets up at 5 A.M. for one of two practices a day. Like, I'm beat because I was at practice and now I have an hour to write a lab report. You use your hour well.

Harrison Macris, sophomore, Boston University

GET THIS! STUDENT-ATHLETES MUST HAVE . . .

- Academic toughness. Getting homework done well (as opposed to just done) requires time management skills all freshmen usually need to work on.
- Physical toughness. The onus is on you to prepare and maintain yourself physically—with maybe one month off a year. You have to know what's achy and what's injured.
- Mental toughness. Enough to focus when you're not in the game, to do homework on Friday night rather than go out, and to stay off the front page of the newspaper for doing something stupid or illegal.

If you want to stay athletic in college, start a routine within days of orientation—and stick to it. It's much more difficult to start midyear. Also, make friends who do the same and will hassle you if you don't show up.

Nathan Pflueger, freshman, Stanford (CA) University

Make sure you have the correct number of credits needed to participate in a sport during a particular season.

Cassius Harris, sophomore, Oberlin (OH) College

In high school I did cross country, track, and soccer. I had way too high expectations for working out that much in college. I'd get frustrated and feel like a failure if I only worked out four times a week instead of six. I had to flip my mental attitude to wanting to work out, even if it was just twice a week, because it was good for me.

Martha Edwards, senior, Marquette University, Milwaukee

> Athletes have mandatory study times, which, actually, the school should do for everybody.
>
> *Elizabeth Pitruzzello, senior, Central Connecticut State University, New Britain*

High school to college was not a big difference, because I went from a small high school to a small juco (junior college). I was on the baseball team to get a free education and to make friends. The big change was from there to OSU. I wasn't on the baseball team here so I didn't have 30 people I knew instantly. I lived off campus, and it was hard to meet people.

Nick Davidson, senior, Oklahoma State University, Stillwater

Intramural and Club Sports

Club sports teams bring a higher level of competition, with set practices, game times, and travel. If you can't perform up to the team's standards because you don't put in the time, you shouldn't join. Intramurals don't have set practices, but there's a high level of competition, actually. It isn't easy to win a tournament, even if you were a high school jock.

Dan Isaacs, junior, State University of New York–Binghamton

Do a sport your first year. It's a great way to make friends. And the exercise makes you happy and releases endorphins. Just sitting around for days, you get more and more lethargic.
Christina Hoffman, junior, Harvard University, Cambridge, MA

I talked to someone on the Ultimate (Frisbee) team and she got me to go to some practices. The team will party together, but they aren't the only people you socialize with. It's more like just one more added social group that you can do stuff with.
Ian Young, sophomore, Grinnell (IA) College

> Intramurals are a great way to learn how to play new sports that you never dreamed you'd play.
>
> *Sara Kaminski, senior, Purdue University, West Lafayette, IN*

After I played almost every intramural sport offered, I realized I couldn't have managed being away from all those friends. In varsity sports, the only friends you're with are on the team.
Jason Kaplan, senior, Colgate University, Hamilton, NY

GET THIS! SOMETHING FUN THAT'S ACTUALLY GOOD FOR YOU

Why signing up for a team is doing yourself a favor:
- Beats sitting around playing video games alone
- Allows you to skip practice when a paper is due
- Fits into the rest of your life instead of being your life
- Lets you go home for holidays instead of lifting and pressing in the weight room
- Takes the edge off and lets you unwind in a healthful way

Although I was a fairly competitive athlete in high school, Amherst is too small to have the sports I used to do. Now I play Ultimate Frisbee, a club sport. I like being on a team while not having to make as serious a time commitment as if I played a varsity sport but still competing and staying in shape and healthy.

Gina Turrini, junior, Amherst (MA) College

GET THIS! QUITTING WITHOUT ANGST

If it really isn't your thing and you're not having fun, quit. Quitting won't be a hardship on everybody else unless it's right before a big game. I tried rugby, and two days into it, I thought I was going to die. I'd heard rugby involved tackling, but I didn't realize it was—tackling!

Rachel Pfennig, freshman, DePauw University, Greencastle, IN

That whole societal thing about once-a-quitter, always-a-quitter is total B.S.

Paul Bromen, junior, St. Olaf College, Northfield, MN

High school football was so competitive. Our fraternity football tournament is just teams of buddies practicing whenever you want to.
Austin Hudson, freshman, Mississippi State University, Starkville

I was on a floor hockey league where most hadn't played since sixth grade. We played a lot of club hockey teams. Our last game, we played against a baseball (turned hockey) team. Their coach was giving them pointers; we were there to have fun.
Will Burton, junior, University of Oregon, Eugene

Going Greek—No, Thanks

My first week at school the question of whether to go Greek or not felt more important and certainly more urgent than picking my major. And I was sure it would impact the rest of my life. I found out it wasn't so important when I decided not to go Greek and then joined a lot of other activities.
Adrienne May, sophomore, University of Missouri–Kansas City

Going Greek requires an incredible commitment—your study time, time with friends, nearly all of your time when you're pledging. I am not going to get out of bed and run around the track for an hour. After that, you're involved in rush, meetings, volunteering, parties, and social events. For me, that was a level of independence I didn't want to sacrifice.
Dan Isaacs, junior, State University of New York–Binghamton

There isn't a Greek system here, and that's one reason I chose this school. I've read about how sororities and fraternities rule the campus, and that you can't do anything about it.
Sandra Lazo de la Vega, sophomore, Florida Atlantic University, Wilkes Honors College, Jupiter

I have good friends who are independent and getting as much out of university life as I am as a Greek.

Graham Shepherd, senior, DePauw University, Greencastle, IN

Frat systems rule, but I'm not in one. I hang around with my roommate and her boyfriend who's on the baseball team. So I've found a place outside the fraternity system.

Jessica Monroe, sophomore, Butler University, Indianapolis, IN

Some people are stereotypical toward fraternities and sororities, and you *will* have to deal with that if you join. For instance, one girl said she didn't like a certain style for our floor T-shirts because it reminded her of the style a sorority had for their shirts. She said if we picked that style she would have to "dye her hair blonde and have sex with a bunch of guys."

Amie Reed, junior, Illinois State University, Normal

I opted out, believing I had better things to do with my time and money than buy a group of "friends" who would humiliate and boss me around for months before finally accepting me as a "brother." Seems like a silly system, but maybe that's just me.

Michael Salvati, junior, Villanova University, Philadelphia

All the sororities have their own personality. With me being a short, brown-haired, Jewish girl, I know the sorority that would pick me and I don't feel like it would suit me.

Laura Polden, freshman, George Washington University, Washington, DC

DID WE MENTION THAT . . .

> One student told us there's enough drama in her life without living in a big house of only girls.

The girl I met during sorority rush has been my roommate for the last two years. I gained a lot of insight into the whole system and understand it better. I'm still glad I didn't pledge because it would have taken a lot of time, and I didn't think the all-female environment was what I was looking for.

Maria Henning, junior, University of California–Berkeley

Hold off on the Greek thing until sophomore year so you get to know your university. At bigger universities, you need to find a social group or you'll get lost, so being Greek defines you more. At a smaller system, people will know you anyway.

Katie Loberg, junior, Loyola University, Chicago

Going Greek—Definitely

I never had a clothes-swapping, story-sharing, girl-to-go-shopping-with sister. A sorority definitely gave me that sisterhood.

Chelsea Chaney, junior, Washburn University, Topeka, KS

I came to an out-of-state school not knowing a soul. This was a great way to meet people day one of my college experience. In a nutshell, sorority life is a family for me in college.

Molly Egan, fourth year of five-year architecture program, University of Tennessee, Knoxville

DID WE MENTION THAT . . .

> It makes a big campus feel so much smaller, especially if you're from out of state. You can walk around all week and not see anyone you know. Then, hey, there's a fraternity/sorority brother/sister and you think, "Oh, yea, a friend."

I grew up in a college town where all you heard about Greeks was negative, like jumping into fountains in the middle of the night. But the guide for my Drake visit was Greek, interesting, and I decided to give it a shot. Every campus is different.

Brianna Orton, senior, Drake University, Des Moines, IA

Fraternities are not what you see in the movies, not just drinking and parties all the time. Yeah, that does take place, but it takes place if you are not in a fraternity, too.

Austin Hudson, freshman, Mississippi State University, Starkville

One of the main things for me was finding one that wasn't totally party oriented. I'm the philanthropy chairman and we volunteer somewhere every couple of months. We helped an older couple move from one place to another. We help with campus Saferide from 10 P.M. to 4 A.M.

Tanner Kokemuller, freshman, Colorado State University, Fort Collins

With service and business organizations, members have particular interests in common. With Greeks, you find people who are not like you. My roommates/sorority sisters' majors are magazine journalism, history, and biology. I'm a finance major.

Brianna Orton, senior, Drake University, Des Moines, IA

BELIEVE IT! *ANIMAL HOUSE* DÉJÀ VU

Every year, on the last day freshmen are required to clean one of the frat houses, they pour Dawn all over the kitchen and dining room floors, dump buckets of water, and do what they call naked beer slides. We always get out the binoculars. Once, one of the guys noticed and came running across the street buck-naked, to get us to come help clean. Finally, some brave girls put on swimming suits and went over. It's not that awkward to have a bunch of naked men slipping and sliding around, but it does teach you eye contact.

Annon Woodin, senior, Iowa State University, Ames

The Greek system is hard-core for freshmen and sophomores. By junior year, it doesn't matter.

Joanna Stone, senior, University of Mississippi, Oxford

Rush Week—Parties, Free Food, and Bonding

If you don't rush, you'll always wonder.

Sage Middleton, senior, Tulane University, New Orleans

It's all free. I didn't pay for a meal that week. You meet a lot of people all at once and everyone likes you and wants you to join.

Tanner Kokemuller, freshman, Colorado State University, Fort Collins

You are in a house for a certain amount of time and all the people helping have synchronized watches. You aren't supposed to talk to them outside of rush, and they chant at you for two minutes. Part of me thinks this is really weird, but I'm still considering joining, so that's probably going to be me next year. Give it a try.

Raija Bushnell, freshman, DePauw University, Greencastle, IN

GET THIS! RUSH WEEK WISDOM

- Getting sloppy drunk before rush parties is a fairly stupid idea if you have your eye on a bid.
- If you pretend to be someone you're not, you'll wind up in a house suited for someone you're not.
- Don't ask, "What are my chances of getting in?"

Even if you do not join, rush is a great way to get to know people. I met one of my best friends in the rush line outside a house, even though we decided to join different sororities.

Ann Nicoletti, junior, Emory University, Atlanta

I attended a Greek organization party with a friend. After we left, she told me to slap her if she ever joined a sorority. Let's just say I slapped her.

Katie Jozwik, junior, Columbia College, Chicago

GET THIS! ANOTHER KIND OF RUSH

I never thought I was going to join a fraternity. One day I met a guy who was dating a girl from my dorm. We hit it off right away. He began inviting me to hang out at his fraternity house. I realized he was rushing me, and while I was still skeptical about joining, I was fine going over there. [Eventually, I pledged, and] while it was sometimes rough and demanding of my time, I don't regret it. They let me pledge dry and never gave me a hard time about it once I was a brother.

Ryan Scofield, senior, College of William & Mary, Williamsburg, VA

I had decided not to rush because Greeks were fake. But half our floor went Greek and they were good friends of mine. So at the end of freshman year, I went through informal rush. If you visit a house three times and they like you, they give you a bid.

Annon Woodin, senior, Iowa State University, Ames

Greek life is definitely shoved in your face the first week. Even I, a lifelong nonsorority girl, was having second thoughts. I ultimately dropped out of rush, but I don't regret a minute of it! I still know girls who I rushed with, and besides, what else are you going to do that first week?

Adrienne May, sophomore, University of Missouri–Kansas City

GET THIS! FIVE WORST REASONS TO GO GREEK

1. Fearing you'll be lonely on weekends that often start right after class on Thursday
2. Wanting access to old exams in the house files
3. Loving the huge house with a view
4. Building a network for when you turn 35 and run for president (of the United States)
5. Caving to pressure from a roommate, friend, sibling, or your parents

If you don't get into a house, it's not like everybody remembers for the rest of your college career. It's not like you'll never have friends. And it's not like Greek people won't hang out with you.

Joanna Stone, senior, University of Mississippi, Oxford

I thought joining a fraternity was a lot of money, and what's the purpose? But I went through rush just to see what it was all about. The people I met changed my mind.

Austin Hudson, freshman, Mississippi State University, Starkville

20/20 HINDSIGHT

Rush is so superficial, but a few sorority girls made it worthwhile. Having small talk with people who were judging me based on how I looked didn't sound appealing. Even so, I did rush and pledged because I found a sorority that was genuine. Hold your breath, go, and hope it gets over soon.

Sage Middleton, senior, Tulane University, New Orleans

GET THIS! HAZING IS NO JOKE

One person's idea of hazing may be another person's "Hey, we're just having a little fun here." Whatever, here's the short scoop.

- Hazing exists (but not everywhere) despite school prohibitions and many states outlawing it.
- Hazing involves abusive tricks or ridicule, such as kneeling for hours, being blindfolded and abandoned far off campus, or ingesting excessive amounts of alcohol.
- Hazing can definitely be harmful to your health, even leading to death.

So how do you deal with hazing?

- Ask around about which fraternities or clubs have lots of drinking or seem abusive or out of control. Students may know more than the administration.
- If the members don't seem authentic, they probably aren't. Trust your instincts.
- Report physical or verbal abuse to your R.A. or a dean and the police.

Hazing is considered anything that excludes one person from another person. We're really strict as a fraternity, and so is the campus as a whole. As a pledge, I didn't do anything any active brother didn't do.
Tanner Kokemuller, freshman, Colorado State University, Fort Collins

Balancing Job and School

If you are looking for a job, always get one around food.
Lindsey Connolly, junior, Arizona State University, Tempe

Balancing work and play is hard because there's no parent around saying, "You can't go out tonight."
Niki Grangruth, senior, St. Olaf College, Northfield, MN

Food service pays better, but I sure would not want to do it, because there's no homework time whatsoever and it's not very challenging or fun unless the co-workers are really fun to be around.

Ian Young, sophomore, Grinnell (IA) College

Get established at school. Then look first for an on-campus job or one where you work a lot on weekends. And pencil in 90 minutes of free time every day, because without that, your grades will be affected.

Jeff Eskew, senior, Texas Christian University, Fort Worth

I recommend not having a job, if possible, because you want to be able to take as many classes as possible and to succeed (and preferably stay awake during them). Especially at a large school, you'll find out by senior year that you haven't taken all the classes you want to! Save the summers for working.

Chris Petz, senior, University of Washington, Seattle

If you work, and go to school, all you do is work-study-work-study. You'll think, "I don't really need to go to classes today because they need me here at work." But you need to go to class more than you need to work. You don't want to pay to retake the class.

Elizabeth Pitruzzello, senior, Central Connecticut State University, New Britain

---

Get a campus job where you can study at work, like the front desk in the dorm. You just sit there and sign when packages come.

Rebecca Zwisler, senior, St. Mary's College, Notre Dame, IN

GET THIS! OVERDRIVE—NOT FOR EVERYONE

▶ I work full time, run my company full time, and take five classes two days a week, so I usually don't have time to socialize with my classmates. Plus, they are stressing out about homework and tests while I am in a hurry to make business meetings and then to work the night shift at the Marriott, so it makes it hard to relate to them.

Konrad Waliszewski, sophomore, American University, Washington, DC

If I'm tired I go to sleep, but I get up and do schoolwork in the morning to keep up. Fifty percent of my time on Thursday through Saturday I stay in and do schoolwork. Most of my friends have jobs and do the same.

Colleen Thurston, junior, University of Arizona, Tucson

I scheduled classes from 10 A.M., and the last one is at 1:30 P.M. every day. It works great because I'm looking into getting a job and it will be easier to say I will be able to work every day at 3 P.M.

James Balkam, freshman, West Virginia University, Morgantown

DID WE MENTION THAT . . .

▶ The *perfect* job description: near or on campus, good pay, flexible scheduling, no surprise added hours, downtime to do homework, access to copier and printer, fun co-workers, provides good references, relates to your possible major(s), challenges your brain, teaches skills that will come in handy later, and free pizza. Okay, you probably won't get the pizza.

If you work off campus, figure out transportation and how it will work with your classes.

Jason Chen, junior, Vassar College, Poughkeepsie, NY

GET THIS! KEYS TO JOB-SCHOOL NIRVANA

- Manage your time really well during the week so you can have free weekends.
- Divide your work and study into separate categories. (And no fair crossing over.)
- Work at something you love.

Bryn Rouse, sophomore, University of Montana, Missoula

I worked at a coffee shop about 20 hours a week, so it was a nice break from thinking about school all the time. Being so busy kept me more focused; if I'm not busy, I get lazy and don't do all the reading.

Jennifer Herlihy, senior, University of California–Berkeley

9

Stay Healthy: Good Food and Bad Colds

Nobody's going to tell you to eat your vegetables anymore, or to turn off the TV, or go outside and play in the fresh air. As if adjusting to college, studying, and making new friends isn't enough, now you're in charge of your diet and health, too. A tall order, especially considering your food fare is primarily cafeteria and your health depends on how the other 59 people on your floor are feeling. About that food: In some cafeterias, it seems everything is deep-fried except the salad. Translation: The Freshman 15 is real (even if it takes two years to acquire). So, too, are hellacious colds, students dragging half dead across campus to take a test, and war stories about the student health center. What to do? Check out the health center before you're sick, eat right, exercise, and get plenty of sleep—none of which may even seem close to possible.

Food Courts, "Sneeze Bars," and Meal Plans

Get the biggest meal plan possible, because you can never eat too much, plus the dorms are hard to cook in.

Abby Beaves, freshman, St. Cloud (MN) State University

The food may seem great for even the first semester, but you will get sick of it! By the end of the year, we were doing everything in our power to avoid the local dining hall. This often meant spending our own hard-earned money on pizza, making the walk to Taco Bell, or ordering Thai at 2 A.M., but it was worth it.

David Neumann, sophomore, University of Southern California, Los Angeles

I come from a family that's big on the whole eating thing. So cafeteria food is disappointing. I live close to one dining hall with an all-you-can-eat buffet that is lesser quality than other dining halls. And lesser quality of cafeteria standards is *really* lesser.

Zack Barr, freshman, Brandeis University, Waltham, MA

We have a midnight breakfast in the cafeteria a couple of nights before finals.

Meghan Hannahs, junior, Westminster College, Salt Lake City

My freshman year I was privileged to attend a school (Illinois State University) with a great cafeteria. We had small restaurants contained in five huge dining centers. As for those who aren't so fortunate, there has to be a Wal-Mart nearby.

Katie Jozwik, junior, Columbia College, Chicago

If you don't have a choice, eat the cafeteria food, then go work out.

Shakira Ali, sophomore, Loyola University, Chicago

GET THIS! (ALMOST) BETTER THAN HOME COOKING

Stephen Hampton, senior, Wheaton (IL) College, e-mailed that his favorite dining hall breakfast is bananas cooked inside a Belgian waffle with strawberries and whipped cream on top. His second-choice favorites include these:

- custom-made omelet with mushrooms, tomatoes, and sausage
- still-soft blueberry bagel with cream cheese
- fresh fruit, yogurt, and homemade granola

Of course Stephen has other meal options:

- pizza—pepperoni, three cheese, meat lovers, or pumpkin marshmallow (really!)
- chilled strawberry soup
- Hawaiian pot roast
- crab salad

And during finals, they put out snacks like Rice Krispies treats so students can grab a chunk as they head off to study.

GET THIS! TOP 10 SCHOOLS WITH THE BEST CAMPUS DINING

1. Scripps College, Claremont, CA
2. Boston University, Boston, MA
3. Cornell University, Ithaca, NY
4. Bryn Mawr College, Bryn Mawr, PA
5. Bowdoin College, Brunswick, ME
6. West Point, West Point, NY
7. University of Notre Dame, South Bend, IN
8. Michigan State University, East Lansing, MI
9. Middlebury College, Middlebury, VT
10. Colby College, Waterville, ME

I tried to eat stuff they couldn't possibly mess up. They did a good job keeping the salad bar fresh, so that was always a safe bet. And there was an awesome selection of cereal, so I ate a lot of that.

Kelly Schroeder, junior, University of Kansas, Lawrence

DID WE MENTION THAT . . .

When you go home:
- Think about how much better that food tastes.
- Seconds are free.
- Your mom (or maybe your dad) will fix whatever you ask for. At least for the first four or five days.

I load up on food from my parents and the dining hall, then save the (meal plan) points. At the end of the semester, I have enough points to go to the restaurant where the president entertains potential donors with lobster and steak.

Mike Husni, junior, University of Delaware, Newark

At first, the dining halls are kind of overwhelming because you can eat whatever, whenever, and as much as you want. You go to the cafeteria for three cheeseburgers or five bowls of cereal. Eventually, that kind of wears off and you stop doing it.

Ross Kaplan, senior, Colby College, Waterville, ME

GET THIS! BREAKFAST CALL

This is hard, but remind yourself to go to breakfast.
Joe Kempf, senior, St. Olaf College, Northfield, MN

If you don't eat breakfast, your brain is not going to get enough blood sugar and you'll start to fade out quicker.
Jesse Herwitz, junior, Fordham University, New York

Sleeping in, then rushing to get ready is one of the worst things you can do as far as your health goes because you don't grab an apple or a banana, you grab a doughnut or breakfast sausage thing. Try getting up 30 minutes earlier. You lose a little sleep, but more time means you'll eat better.
Jennifer Bowen, sophomore, Westminster College, Salt Lake City

It's impossible to eat right and healthy when your food court has Taco Bell and Burger King.

Fadi Bayaa, junior, California State University–Long Beach

GET THIS! AMAZING, BUT TRUE

When one student told the food services director the gravy (as in biscuits and gravy), wasn't up to par, the director sought him out a week later to ask if he was pleased with the changes they had made. We are not kidding about this.

I used to go to the dining hall a lot but stopped because I went on the Web site one day and found all that high-calorie food, and after awhile you just get sick of it.

Diane Hennan, freshman, Saint Ambrose University, Davenport, IA

GET THIS! SARAH SURVIVES THE DINING HALL BY . . .

- Choosing different options to vary her diet. It gets really boring to eat cereal every morning.
- Keeping some cafeteria food like bagels and fruit for later.
- Making a PBJ or doing a "grab-and-go sandwich" if nothing looks good.
- Eating with different groups in the cafeteria or getting together with people to cook a meal away from the neon lights, crowds, and plastic trays.

Sarah Sentz, sophomore, University of Montana, Missoula

It's really easy to complain about the dining hall, so remember, you don't have somebody making you custom omelets at home.

Emily Cullings, junior, Colgate University, Hamilton, NY

Where's the Best Free Food?

Girls' rooms. They're always full of snacks. The girls say, "My parents sent all this food and I don't want to eat it by myself." If you're a guy, they'll share with you.

Joe Kempf, senior, St. Olaf College, Northfield, MN

Back home. My roommate's mom makes apple fritters, wraps them up and my roommate brings back a stock that lasts for two weeks. My favorite food is Doritos. When I come back, they say, "I smell Doritos." Your popularity rises.

Emily Cullings, junior, Colgate University, Hamilton, NY

DID WE MENTION THAT . . .

Organizers bribe students to come to meetings by offering food. If the sponsor is a cultural organization, bonus time—they'll have food you wouldn't ordinarily get.

The Women's Center (at my first college). We had a lot of free potlucks. The homemade foods tasted better and the atmosphere was better than the cafeteria.

Sarah Sentz, sophomore, University of Montana, Missoula

Professors' invites. Some meet with their students for coffee or breakfast. Or they have the class to their house for dinner, or take everyone to an on-campus restaurant. You just eat and chat. It's nice.

Emily Gravett, senior, Colgate University, Hamilton, NY

Twinkies and Junk Food—a Basic Food Group?

Twinkies? Definitely. Absolutely. There isn't much space in your room, maybe no fridge, one kitchen for the whole building, and no time to cook. You're hungry and can't get to the dining hall so you have these Twinkies, which are better than nothing.

Dan Isaacs, junior, State University of New York–Binghamton

Upperclassmen all watch freshmen line up at the soft-serve machine. They laugh because they lined up at the soft-serve machine, too.

Christine Fletcher, junior, Bates College, Lewiston, ME

> Most people recognize they have a problem with eating Twinkies. They just don't feel like they have an alternative. Twinkies are so cheap.
>
> *Fadi Bayaa, junior, California State University–Long Beach*

GET THIS! SHOCKING NEWS

▶ Personal experience teaches unsuspecting freshmen that
- once you stop eating those burgers for a while, you won't ever be able to eat them again;
- you can buy a meal of ramen noodles for 15 cents, but carbs and salt (read that as "weight") come with it.

I was drinking about 12 sodas a day, went cold turkey and lost 30 pounds. It was hard the first couple of weeks. Now, three years later, I maybe have a craving once every three months.

Jeff Eskew, senior, Texas Christian University, Fort Worth

That Nasty "Freshman 15"

When you walk across that graduation stage in high school, your metabolism stays behind.

Joanna Stone, senior, University of Mississippi, Oxford

I noticed that people who drank a lot tended to gain weight.

Martha Edwards, senior, Marquette University, Milwaukee

DID WE MENTION THAT . . .

▶ A student we know says to watch out! The Freshman 15 afflicted her more in sophomore year because as things got more stressful, she ate more. Lots more. She's not the only one. Studies show that it's the "freshman five to seven" plus the "sophomore two or three" that nudge you toward the unwanted 15.

My roommate boycotted the dining hall second semester, and I wasn't rooming near anyone else who went there, so I kind of got into a bad habit with junk food. I gained the Freshman 15, and I didn't quite lose it all over the summer.

Tyler Sloss, sophomore, Duke University, Durham, NC

GET THIS! STRANGEST REWARD FOOD

Chocolate-covered ants make a tasty snack or dessert. Be sure to refrigerate leftovers.

Some people see food as a reward. When you are an athlete, food is more a necessity. You know you can't put junk food in your body because it won't be used efficiently.

Harrison Macris, sophomore, Boston University

Menus are online here, so you can check all the calcium, calories, and fat for a meal before you eat. Even though a lot of food is cooked in fatty oils, the important thing is getting fresh fruits and vegetables, and for girls, getting enough protein. Skipping meals, snacking, and going to Burger King are way more unhealthy than dining hall food.

Laura MacLean, senior, University of Notre Dame (IN)

GET THIS! ENERGY TO GET YOU THROUGH THE DULLEST CLASS

Students' unscientifically tested and approved suggestions:

1. Six little meals throughout the day speed up your metabolism and increase your energy.
2. Don't eat past 8 p.m.
3. If you want something that's fast, go to Subway.
4. Make a mix that includes nuts, dried berries, raisins, and M&M's—more energy than a candy bar, unless you just pick out the M&M's.

Club hockey was the best thing I did freshman year. In high school, P.E. forces you to be active. In college, you only have two hours of required P.E., and that's where the Freshman 15 comes in.

Ande Davis, senior, Washburn University, Topeka, KS

20/20 HINDSIGHT

I didn't eat in the cafeteria at first because of the notion that I was going to gain the Freshman 15. So I bought food at an off-campus grocery store to eat in my room. I actually lost about 12 pounds. But I realized the monetary cost of not eating at the cafeteria was too high.

Olamide Oduyingbo, freshman, Quinnipiac University, Hamden, CT

After even a semester of college, I asked myself, "Why did I gain weight?" Then, I said, "Whoa! Burgers and pizza."

Cassius Harris, sophomore, Oberlin (OH) College

DID WE MENTION THAT . . .

▶ Maybe, just maybe, the dryer is shrinking your clothes.

Don't have a two-hour lunch in your class schedule. I did, so I went to the buffet every day and that's when I found out the Freshman 15 is not a myth. I started scheduling activity classes like swimming, tennis, bowling. When there is nothing to do, you eat.

Jeff Eskew, senior, Texas Christian University, Fort Worth

You don't realize you're getting a little chunky until you visit your family. They say, "Oh, you're eating good." No. You're eating horrible.

Shakira Ali, sophomore, Loyola University, Chicago

R.A.s Talk About Eating Disorders

As an R.A. specializing in women's issues this past year, I have definitely encountered several women who have been dealing with anorexia and bulimia. There is open discourse about the issue, and people like us are key in identifying those who might be at risk or who do have an eating disorder.

Sri Kalyanaraman, junior, Brown University, Providence, RI

We have single-gender dorms, and there are unique problems in an all-female environment. One of the hardest problems is eating disorders. Here, many girls are used to being the best at anything they do, including being in good shape. There are girls who are working out constantly, skipping meals, and living on coffee and carrot sticks. It's almost impossible to see or approach a girl unless her roommate, boyfriend, or friends report her behavior. People close to that person need to go to an R.A. to get help for her.

Laura MacLean, senior, R.A., University of Notre Dame, IN

BELIEVE IT! WHEN SIZE 0 SEEMS TOO BIG

The summer before college, I became lactose intolerant, which messed up my eating. I lost a little weight and people said, "You look good." I thought, "I must be fat." By the time college started, I wouldn't eat in front of people. I was living at home and my mom worked all day, so at night, I'd just say, "Oh, I ate earlier." I transferred here sophomore year and not eating was harder to hide. My roommate would say, "Hey, let's go eat." She was small like me, but she was eating. I'd bought a size 0 pants and thought, "They must be huge because I can fit in them." I began to realize this was ridiculous, stupid. I can't say I don't ever think about my weight sometimes. Everyone does, especially college girls, because everyone else is so much smaller and prettier. But you just have to be okay with yourself. You are never going to be perfect. That will help. So will getting involved in an activity. I joined the newspaper staff and instead of worrying about weighing 100 pounds, I started thinking about becoming the editor.

Julie Ledbetter, senior, Clemson (SC) University (where she is editor of The Clemson Tiger)

Exercise Beyond Climbing One Flight of Stairs

You will be walking everywhere. At first, you'll be surprised at how out-of-shape you are.

Brittany Borstad, junior, Iowa State University, Ames

Get into a routine of doing the same thing at a specific time, like play ball every Thursday or run every Wednesday.

James Balkam, freshman, West Virginia University, Morgantown

Regular exercise is easier if you have friends who motivate each other or if you have to meet people at the gym.

Christine Fletcher, junior, Bates College, Lewiston, ME

I go to the gym four or five times a week, and realized I really enjoy running. Now, I've run the Philadelphia and Boston marathons.

Christina Hoffman, junior, Harvard University, Cambridge, MA

DID WE MENTION THAT . . .

Students tell us that to keep your resolve to exercise, you have to exercise before downtime hits. After that, you can pretty much talk yourself out of anything that requires physical effort, unless it's to run out of a burning building.

The elliptical machines boosted my energy, especially in the cold Erie winters when bundling up to make your way to the Athletic Center was a workout in itself.

Jackie Kohler, sophomore, Mercyhurst College, Erie, PA

After researching or revising a paper, go for a walk and take along a note-pad. Think about what you've been working on and jot down notes.

Jade Hidle, senior, California State University–Long Beach

GET THIS! SMOKING IS NOT EXERCISE

A lot of kids smoke cigarettes. Mainly, I think it is an image thing.

Harrison Macris, sophomore, Boston University

It seems like everybody smokes. Nobody watches those public service announcements—the cool "truth" commercials made by and targeted to young people, warning about the dangers of smoking. It's a social thing, and generally some think it is easier to make friends if you do smoke. I thought that my generation would know better. My mom had such a hard time quitting.

Sandra Lazo de la Vega, sophomore, Florida Atlantic University, Wilkes Honors College, Jupiter

If you used to play sports in high school and won't in college, your body will be like, "Keep eating. Keep eating." But you cannot eat the same way, and 10 or 15 pounds will creep up on you.

Joanna Stone, senior, University of Mississippi, Oxford

After I lost 12 pounds and was staying at that weight, I figured that instead of dieting I would change my eating habits, eat more moderately, and exercise regularly. Once you are not thinking about it, that's when you lose weight. But after a while, you just say, "I don't care anymore" and eat a bunch.

Olamide Oduyingbo, freshman, Quinnipiac University, Hamden, CT

> A lot of people leave for the gym at 10 P.M. That seems really late when you are home, but at school, it's normal.
>
> *Lauren Press, junior, University of Denver*

I Was So Sick ...

I didn't have money for a box of tissues, so one day, when my nose was running, I left class, went to the bathroom, and came back with a roll of toilet paper. The teacher said if I was that sick, I should go home.

Jade Hidle, senior, California State University–Long Beach

DID WE MENTION THAT . . .

If you look like the living dead, it's distracting because the teacher and other students are wondering if you are going to live.

GET THIS! THE TRUTH ABOUT BEING SICK AT SCHOOL

- Sickness spreads faster than a good rumor because you're packed together in classes and residence halls.
- Your immune system is timed to break down at midterm and semester finals.
- You can cut class—if you haven't already used up your cuts.
- Don't expect to be given missing work; you have a syllabus and a friend whose notes you can copy.
- You can whine and whimper to your real friends and they'll bring you soup.
- It's not nearly as "nice" as being sick at home in your own bed. Parents bring you juice and say, "Is there anything else you want?" At school, you just keep going, going, going. No wonder it takes forever to get well!

One suitemate brought pinkeye from another dorm and then my roommate got it. Luckily, I did not get it. We were very careful about washing our hands and things we all touched.

Katie Beno, freshman, Gonzaga University, Spokane, WA

I'm a broadcast journalism major, and once I completely lost my voice. My mom had to come and drive me home because I wouldn't let myself get better at school. After that, I learned to schedule free time.

Jeff Eskew, senior, Texas Christian University, Fort Worth

Staying Healthy Without Dr. Mom Around

Whatever your mother told you to do when you get sick, do it. Vitamin C, drink lots of water, whatever—do it.

Rachel Lenz, junior, Vassar College, Poughkeepsie, NY

Key experiences really strengthen your bond. Like when my roommate broke her nose playing volleyball and we spent three hours in the emergency room.

Raija Bushnell, freshman, DePauw University, Greencastle, IN

DID WE MENTION THAT . . .

You don't have to memorize the government's food pyramid to know how to eat well. You just get an individualized plan at mypyramid.com. Unfortunately, chocolate chips are not on the plan.

If you feel like you are getting sick, the worst thing you can do is go out and drink.

Christina Hoffman, junior, Harvard University, Cambridge, MA

GET THIS! STUDENTS' FAVORITE HOME REMEDIES

- Eat lots of fruits and vegetables.
- Gobble vitamins, especially if you're a junk food king or queen.
- Do laundry regularly to prevent a tower of germs—ugh.
- Rub on hand sanitizer, a lot.
- Use a lip balm stick rather than a pot you stick your finger in.
- Drink OJ every day.
- Put honey in hot tea like your mom makes.
- Guzzle water, not soda or beer, to hydrate and flush your system.

In high school, you eat supper, study, go to bed, and get a good night's sleep. In college, you don't have that schedule. So listen to your body. If you haven't slept for the last two nights and your body tells you you're getting sick, you probably are.

Lauren Press, junior, University of Denver

DID WE MENTION THAT . . .

You study like an idiot, drink coffee, beer, and soda instead of eating salad/vegetables/meat, do not sleep for 48 hours, and suddenly tests and papers are all done. So you relax—and that's when you get sick.

I know you want to stay up at all hours of the night, but *don't do that*. If you don't get at least six hours of sleep a night, you will wear yourself down. Trust me on this, I know, and I got sick.

Alissa Busha, senior, University of Central Oklahoma, Oklahoma City

GET THIS! ONE MORE EXCUSE TO NOT SLEEP

Motorcades used to wake us up in the middle of the night, and we'd rush to the window to see. Now we're really annoyed by them. The president's always going by in his motorcade. It's just about made me into a liberal.

Laura Polden, freshman, George Washington University, Washington, DC

When Chicken Soup Isn't Enough

In Providence, my asthma resurfaced due to the weather. However, the staff at the Health Services was wonderful and has been very kind every time I have gone in. I also discovered one of the Achilles' heels regarding the Health Services: they're not open during spring break!!!! How crazy! Here I am very sick with pneumonia and there is no health place open.

Sri Kalyanaraman, junior, Brown University, Providence, RI

The health center gave me a paper bag with ibuprofen, cough drops, and Sudafed. There's not a lot they can do except call your professors to excuse your absence from class.

Caitlin Wells, sophomore, Grinnell (IA) College

I was sick for two months with a tonsil problem. I had different insurance than FSU's insurance, so I had to pay out-of-pocket for my prescriptions or tests at the campus health center. You can go back and get them to help you reclaim the cost, but who does that? So before you get sick, check if the health center takes your insurance, and if not, find a walk-in clinic off campus that will.

Aimee Ludlow, sophomore, Florida State University, Tallahassee

DID WE MENTION THAT . . .

A student from a religiously-affiliated school told us that when she tried to get her birth control prescription filled at the health center, two nurses took her to a room, closed the door, and grilled her on why she had the prescription. She had to have a medical reason for them to agree to honor her doctor's prescription.

I was getting sick regularly, so I finally went to the health center. It was the greatest thing ever. You go, they check you out and write you a prescription.

Emily Gravett, senior, Colgate University, Hamilton, NY

You might be able to go to a free clinic for tests. Some clinics take the poor, the underprivileged, and college students.

Rebecca Zwisler, senior, St. Mary's College, Notre Dame, IN

10

Love, Sex, Alcohol, and Drugs

You've heard the wild tales of college as party central: binge drinking; hooking up with whomever, wherever, and whenever; going to class high, when students go to class at all. Sure, it happens, and although it's not the norm, it's impossible to ignore. Drinking and drugs are prevalent, and the issues accompanying them magnify the riskier side of college life. Date rape is a reality. Kids get sick. Some flunk out. A few die. You decrease the risk when you have friends upon whom you can depend. You also recognize that you have choices ranging from walking on the wild side to walking on by. Despite any peer pressure, you can find your niche and be true to yourself. And not to belabor the obvious, but it may be best not to tell all when you're back home. This is the stuff that does parents in.

You Really Still Love Your High School Sweetheart?

I wish I would have come in with freedom to date around instead of with a long-term boyfriend. There's a lot of exploring going on, and I wasn't able to do that. At 18, you aren't looking for a life partner; you're looking for a good time.

Emily Gravett, senior, Colgate University, Hamilton, NY

I have been discouraged by parents and friends saying that long-distance relationships don't work out. We have been going together three years. We visit each other two or three times a semester. Don't say you should break up. Try it and see.

Tanner Kokemuller, freshman, Colorado State University, Fort Collins

Feelings change. If you think the relationship may not be working anymore, the other person may be thinking that, too. Two 18-year-olds usually cannot continue a relationship when they are hours away from each other. That sucks, because we like to think we have it all figured out.

Alan Kistler, senior, Fordham University, New York

GET THIS! JOHN'S STAYING-TOGETHER FORMULA

I'm a fifth-year senior and am still with my high school girlfriend, who's in Kansas City. Work at making a relationship grow, because you are completely different people at 18 than at 22 or 23. Long-distance relationships mean a lot of phone conversations. An hour a day? Two hours? Enough to meet each other's emotional needs. Find new ways to show affection, like sending flowers or making unannounced trips. Reinforce that you are still faithful, even though you are at school with 15,000 girls. One way is to have her stay a weekend with you so she can see what you do when you go out. I hang out with my guy friends, so she knew I wasn't just running around with 50 girls she didn't know.

John Schmidt, senior, University of Kansas, Lawrence

If you think the relationship is going to last, go with it. I knew when I was a freshman here that the relationship I still had with my high school boyfriend was rocky, and why I continued with it, I'm not quite sure.

Brianna Orton, senior, Drake University, Des Moines, IA

I was especially homesick because I have this long-distance relationship from high school. We have been dating four years. I have no desire to go to fraternity parties and dances where you grind on a guy and walk away or have a fling. I want something more meaningful. If it's true love and meant to be, it will be.

Erin Pirruccello, sophomore, University of Pennsylvania, Wharton School, Philadelphia

---

I stayed with my high school boyfriend through my freshman year here. I really was grateful we were together because so many things changed in college, and it was a stabilizing thing. It's someone to be there who is not your parents. It was difficult, though, because he lived 45 minutes away.

Maria Henning, junior, University of California–Berkeley

We had a four-to-five-hour long-distance relationship all last year. I went away every two weeks to visit him or he'd visit me. I still met a lot of people on campus with intramurals and dorm events. I could have done that this year, too. But I transferred to Central because of finding more classes in my major, making the softball team, and my boyfriend being there.

Melissa Triber, sophomore, Central Washington University, Ellensburg, WA

I think a lot of girls come to college thinking they have to have a boyfriend. I'm glad I didn't date anybody my freshman year, because that's when you develop friendships.

Chelsea Chaney, junior, Washburn University, Topeka, KS

GET THIS! YOU KNOW IT'S BREAKUP TIME WHEN . . .

- One night everything explodes and you wind up yelling at each other. The next night, it happens again.
- You'll be away from each other for more than a year. And neither of you seems to mind.
- You're determined to keep your long-distance relationship intact, but Vegas won't give you good odds.
- Your normally happy roommate complains, "Enough! No more what-should-I-do-about-my-relationship talk."
- You notice that other students are just as cute—maybe even cuter.

If the relationship is not that strong and you're in it more because of a physical attraction rather than love, the relationship won't withstand the change of you going to college.

Katy Cortese, freshman, University of Kansas, Lawrence

My parents gave me a Web cam to be able to see and talk to them. I gave my boyfriend (at another college) a Web cam. It's better because we can see each other and it saves on phone bills.

Rachel Lenz, junior, Vassar College, Poughkeepsie, NY

20/20 HINDSIGHT

I was away from home for the first time, and I had a boyfriend for the first time. He was at another college, but my grades dropped and I didn't care about college. I put all my effort into my boyfriend. I had to work very, very hard to get my grades up, and it was not an easy journey. I don't care if you have a boyfriend–focus on school. I had to learn the hard way.

Alissa Busha, senior, University of Central Oklahoma, Oklahoma City

20/20 HINDSIGHT

If you're at different schools, it's hard to balance the relationship time with your life at college. When will you visit? Find time to talk? Phone conversations weren't enough. [We broke up] but then saw each other last summer and decided to give it another chance. We've both matured and know what to expect. I wouldn't advise anyone to break up with a high school sweetheart, but realize the time commitment. If you go into college thinking you are not going to have this new life, not going to change, you aren't being realistic.

Katie Loberg, junior, Loyola University, Chicago

Hanging Out, Hooking Up, and (Sometimes) Dating

Casual relationships, hooking up, and dating are pretty equal.

Dan Isaacs, junior, State University of New York, Binghamton

Hanging out is when you're doing normal college-kids' stuff—going to the library, or movies, sitting around talking, being goofy. Hooking up is what happens when everybody leaves except that one person and you. That brings out the term *shacker*. Guys can't stay at sorority houses, so the girl is usually the shacker. It's always a big joke, because in the morning she does the walk of shame back to the house even if it's been an innocent shacker experience.

Annon Woodin, senior, Iowa State University, Ames

No matter whether you like it, you don't like it, you haven't had it, you have had it, you had it and don't do it that much anymore, you had it and now have it like a bunny—get used to it, because it happens, and it happens a lot.

Luke Roth, freshman, Loyola University, Chicago

DID WE MENTION THAT . . .

- If you just hook up with someone, you cannot go around later announcing that your relationship is over and that you've dumped so-and-so. Even short-term relationships last longer than that. (Don't they?)
- If you hook up with someone, then ignore that person and later want to go out with a friend of said hookup, will you look like the jerk you maybe are?
- If you hook up with anyone, are you using a condom?

Making out is part of the freshman experience. You have to make mistakes for yourself or you are never going to learn. Like you think maybe you could have just gone home by yourself that one night, and you might have regrets later. But I actually met my current boyfriend through his roommate, who was one of those randoms. You never know how it's going to turn out.

Brianna Orton, senior, Drake University, Des Moines, IA

Be honest with whomever you are in a relationship about what you will accept and what you want out of the relationship. Listen to your instincts. You must feel good about what's happening or you need to be talking to someone about it.

Laura MacLean, senior, University of Notre Dame (IN)

Be very, very careful. You go out to party, get drunk, and he can be so charming. You think they want what you want, but all they want is to hook up. In the end you realize you're being walked on, and it hurts you and it's not beneficial to get into that kind of behavior.

Aimee Ludlow, sophomore, Florida State University, Tallahassee

Get over the preconceptions that come from movies. Random sex is not that wonderful.

Kevin Spahn, senior, University of Minnesota–Minneapolis

While casual sex may be socially acceptable and sometimes even nice, it can have a lot of unforeseen emotional drawbacks. Still, it varies from one person to the next; sex means something different for different types of people.

Alix Lifka-Reselman, freshman, Brandeis University, Waltham, MA

> I enjoyed freshman year. Lots of meeting people, hooking up, and shameful walks home. But it's all part of the college experience.
>
> *Anonymous*

Sometimes, you may know more about a boy than your girlfriend does. If we think the boy is not a good influence, we bang on the door and say, "Hey, Jane. I'm feeling really sick. Can you come get me some medicine?" It's a support net because you don't want your friends to get hurt.

Raija Bushnell, freshman, DePauw University, Greencastle, IN

DID WE MENTION THAT . . .

▶ When you have a girlfriend/boyfriend who also lives in your hall or dorm, it's called "hallcest."

On some campuses, there isn't a casual dating scene. You go from holding hands to a serious relationship in a week.

Paul Bromen, junior, St. Olaf College, Northfield, MN

I had a girlfriend here four days after getting to campus. It affected my social life. I didn't make a lot of good, close friends you see every day until junior year. When I got into my major—packaging, which is a very social major—I found a group of people and made new friends.

Greg Vanker, senior, Michigan State University, East Lansing

Fraternity boys target freshman girls. You can go out with them, but be sure you know them well first.

Chelsea Chaney, junior, Washburn University, Topeka, KS

In college, all your adolescent bullshit goes out the window. You let the other person know if you like them. Sometimes, it's kind of facilitated by beer.

Rebecca Zwisler, senior, St. Mary's College, Notre Dame, IN

Frank Talk About Date Rape

If a girl and guy have a couple of drinks at a party and make out, and if it looks like this might go farther, err on the side of caution. I know a guy unjustly accused of date rape. It didn't go to trial, but my friend became more cautious and a little paranoid about how he portrayed himself to other people.

Alan Kistler, senior, Fordham University, New York

Be aware of the reality of date rape. For some reason freshmen girls think "that's not going to happen to me," but don't think like that, because you won't be as cautious.

Aimee Ludlow, sophomore, Florida State University, Tallahassee

The worst thing that can happen to you as a freshman is sexual assault. And it happens a lot. Guys prey on girls from small towns because they are naive.

Sage Middleton, senior, Tulane University, New Orleans

Sometimes people want to press charges, but a school may want to handle it privately. Date rape can really give schools a bad name.

Rebecca Zwisler, senior, St. Mary's College, Notre Dame, IN

DID WE MENTION THAT . . .

The real world is not always like a fairy tale where everybody lives happily ever after. The reality is that date rape happens, more often than you think, and you can't just wish it away. So you should know this:

- Date rape is forced, manipulated, nonconsensual sexual activity between acquaintances, friends, people dating, or even in a relationship. Estimates vary, but some indicate that as many as one in four college women has been raped.
- Date rape is predicated on force—from you being overpowered to your partner threatening to spread rumors if you don't have sex.
- "No" is *always* a legitimate response, no matter your past history with this person, what you're wearing, or what you agreed to earlier.
- Date rape drugs can be slipped into food, drink, or even chewing gum. They can cause aggressive behavior, loss of inhibition, drowsiness, inability to communicate, amnesia, hallucinations, unconsciousness, and even death.
- Alcohol is like a date-rape drug, and binge drinking is a primary instigator, because it's harder to note if a situation is dangerous and easier to succumb to sexual or physical assault.

So, Where's the Party?

You're coming from high school, where a social structure was established, to college, where there is not yet a social structure. The first thing you'll want to do is make associations and build small groups. The most common way is to go drinking or get together and get stoned. Just make sure you control the situation and that it doesn't control you. And if it's something you don't want to do, don't do it.

Kevin Spahn, senior, University of Minnesota–Minneapolis

Don't go off the deep end just because you're on your own for the first time. A lot of people go out every night, which I wouldn't suggest, and don't do schoolwork and flunk out.

Austin Hudson, freshman, Mississippi State University, Starkville

I'm happy I didn't choose the real party dorm. I'm in one that has a great party life but not insane. It's great to be social all the time, but I would flunk out of school if I did that. When you pay so much money to learn, you might as well just learn.

Laura Polden, freshman, George Washington University, Washington, DC

My parents never gave me a curfew. They were trusting and loving. I did all my stupidity and experimenting in high school. I felt free my whole life, so I wasn't intoxicated by the idea of no one controlling me when I came to college.

Leor Benyamini, junior, Quinnipiac University, Hamden, CT

GET THIS! PARTY POINTERS

- Even if you aren't a party animal, show up at a few parties early on just to meet new people. That's why everyone else is there, too.
- Do not party-hop alone.
- Anyone extremely intoxicated may be in danger—of dying, actually.
- Know the party's location in case your "friends" leave you there.
- If you're sober and everyone else is not, your entertainment might become watching them until about 10:30, when they think they are funny and you no longer do.
- If you're wasted and black out, how will you know if you had fun?

Older kids pressure freshmen at frat parties into drinking a whole lot. A lot of my friends just got really fat from massive amounts of cheap beer.

James Langlois, junior, Tulane University, New Orleans

GET THIS! TOP 10 BEST NIGHTLIFE COLLEGES

1. New York University, New York, NY
2. Louisiana State University, Baton Rouge, LA
3. Loyola Marymount University, Los Angeles, CA
4. Tulane University, New Orleans, LA
5. University of Southern California, Los Angeles, CA
6. Arizona State University, Tempe, AZ
7. University of Miami, Coral Gables, FL
8. McGill University, Montreal, QC
9. Loyola University–New Orleans, New Orleans, LA
10. Occidental College, Los Angeles, CA

Before you go to a frat party, make sure you know at least one of the boys and what band is playing. If the band turns out to have dirty girls dancing on stage, chances are you will not want to be there that long. Therefore, you just wasted your time. (This happened to me before. *Nasty!*)

Lauren Krpan, sophomore, University of Mississippi, Oxford

I hate frat parties. You can watch amazing students turn into very foolish people in a matter of hours.

Sri Kalyanaraman, junior, Brown University, Providence, RI

I partied a little to reward myself for a job well done. When I became legal, things changed and I began to explore the bar scene more than anything else.

Jennifer Herlihy, senior, University of California–Berkeley

Don't think of college as a party place away from home; think of it as the place where you get ready for the rest of your life.

Jennifer Bowen, sophomore, Westminster College, Salt Lake City

Whether it's about going on a date or drinking at a party, everyone else is also anxious; no one is invincible. Once you observe them and think about that, you get some form of understanding that you are not alone.

Clark Young, freshman, Georgetown University, Washington, DC

GET THIS! YOU NEED TO KNOW ...

the people you are drinking with if you are going to get plastered. And don't get plastered if you go to a party.

Maria Henning, junior, University of California–Berkeley

how to handle a situation that involves cops at a party. Colleges have *a lot* of cops and they always seem to find the big parties, so be careful.

Amie Reed, junior, Illinois State University, Normal

yourself and what you want. Some students prefer to sacrifice grades to have a good time. I'm more future oriented.

Cristina Baptista, graduate student, Fordham University, Bronx, NY

My experience is that people are usually good about watching out for friends. If someone has drunk too much, a couple of people will watch them the rest of the night to make sure they are not really, really sick.

Ian Young, sophomore, Grinnell (IA) College

20/20 HINDSIGHT

You get to reinvent yourself in college. In high school I did things I didn't want to do, and that carried over to first semester of college. I made bad choices, hooked up with guys, was messy, drinking too much. I decided to change. I'm trying new things, like rugby and getting back into photography. I'm finding the nerdy Alix, finding myself. I have actually reverted to an earlier me. I don't need to change to make friends, so I change to make me happy with myself.

Alix Lifka-Reselman, freshman, Brandeis University, Waltham, MA

Beer as Nutrition, Wine in a Box, Mixed Drinks in a Garbage Can

Anyone who comes into college not knowing very much about drinking is going to get hard-core exposed. On a smaller campus in a small town, everyone drinks because there is nothing better to do on the weekend. Always realize you have a choice. You'll be okay if you say no.

Brittany Borstad, junior, Iowa State University, Ames

Freshmen have to learn their own tolerance for alcohol. They don't realize they are doing too much alcohol until they are doing it.

Rachel Lenz, junior, Vassar College, Poughkeepsie, NY

A police officer found a freshman friend of mine passed out in the yard of a fraternity house. He was taken to the hospital, and I picked him up there later. He had to call his parents the next morning to pay the hospital bill and confess about his drinking. His parents didn't even know he drank.

Joanna Stone, senior, University of Mississippi, Oxford

> Everyone gets really, really drunk one time, and then really, really sick the next morning. Maybe more than once.
>
> *Ross Kaplan, senior, Colby College, Waterville, ME*

DID WE MENTION THAT . . .

All the songs about drinking won't tell you this part.

1. Freshman make up 24 percent of students enrolled in four-year institutions, but they account for 35 percent of student deaths, with almost one-third caused by an alcohol or drug overdose.
2. It used to be a guy thing, but now women are drinking more, and more are binge drinking on purpose.
3. You can die from drinking too much too fast.

People would rather be with the guy who can have two drinks and hang out and talk about life than the person who throws back 10 beers or shots, then tries to fly off the table. And you don't prove anything by throwing up.

Alan Kistler, senior, Fordham University, New York

I got punched in the boob at a basketball game by a drunk kid. A bit later he got in a fight with someone and got what was coming to him.

Laura Polden, freshman, George Washington University, Washington, DC

You can have one drink at a party and not have to hang out there too long. People don't remember you the next day anyway. And it's more fun pretending you're drunk.

Meghan Hannahs, junior, Westminster College, Salt Lake City

GET THIS! ACCORDING TO AMIE . . .

- Drinking tickets are not cheap.
- Things can happen that you won't remember in the morning.

Amie Reed, junior, Illinois State University, Normal

If you are with friends who all are drunk, no one will help you. I don't like the taste of alcohol. I'm usually the one who will watch over my friends, like a little mother hen.

Olamide Oduyingbo, freshman, Quinnipiac University, Hamden, CT

Please be careful where you drink and who you drink with. A lot of college guys are looking to take advantage and have sex.

Sage Middleton, senior, Tulane University, New Orleans

Don't trust people in a bar, not their intentions, words, or actions. At least be conscious of what can happen.

Leor Benyamini, junior, Quinnipiac University, Hamden, CT

Avoid mixed drinks in a garbage can because you don't know what's in there. I didn't realize this until I got to college, but people may be allergic to certain types of alcohol or to the grains in beer. You can keep your drinks cheap, but that doesn't mean you have to drink swill.

Kevin Spahn, senior, University of Minnesota–Minneapolis

GET THIS! STUDENTS TELL US THAT ...

- there's a time to drink and a time to study and you need to know that line;
- four cups of beer can equal six or seven beers;
- jungle juice in those little kiddy pools tastes just as wicked as mixes in garbage cans.

My group loves to party. I usually keep myself in check because I have a relatively low tolerance for alcohol. I forget things I did even when I'm sober.

Clark Young, freshman, Georgetown University, Washington, DC

Coming from a conservative family who probably wouldn't be happy to hear me say this, you have very little to lose by at least trying it. You don't need to go overboard and be the biggest drinker at the party. But to completely abstain is either foolish or somebody with very good morals.

Will Burton, junior, University of Oregon, Eugene

Why do you need a fake ID? If the party's over at 1 A.M. and the bar closes at 2 A.M., what's going to happen in that hour?

Katie Loberg, junior, Loyola University, Chicago

BELIEVE IT! STUDENT WAKES UP IN THE E.R.

I've had some bad experience with drinking. On Halloween, I got alcohol poisoning and had to go to the hospital emergency room. I was with some people I don't really hang out with that much. I had a lot of liquor real fast, blacked out about 8 P.M., and woke up the next morning in the E.R. It's almost a given that wherever you go in college there will be alcohol, and you must know when you need to stop. Know what's right for you. I have been attending mandatory alcohol awareness program classes and doing community service by working at the Ronald McDonald House near the hospital. My parents knew all about my alcohol poisoning, and I talked to them about it later. Another bad part: I collected a whole bunch of medical bills, ambulance, doctors, totaling about $1,000. I've paid off the bills and submitted a claim to my insurance. But so far, it's out of my pocket.

James Balkam, freshman, West Virginia University, Morgantown

For my birthday, my friends wanted to take me out to celebrate. I was fed shots of sambuca and, in the morning, I couldn't get out of bed. Friends and family were calling to wish me a happy birthday while my head was stuck in the garbage can. If you're going to celebrate, don't do it with hard liquor.

Anonymous

GET THIS! BINGE DRINKING 101

Part A

- It's generally considered binge drinking when men drink five or more alcoholic drinks—for women it's four or more—at a party or alone.
- Drinking alcohol, even without binge drinking, can make you behave like a jerk, harm every organ in your body, and cause you to forget what happened or pass out.
- Alcohol is a downer, so if you were depressed before you drank, you won't be feeling better afterward.
- Mixing it with other drugs—even some over-the-counter drugs—can kill you.

Part B

If you have a friend who is hung over a lot, has to drink to have fun, lies about how much he/she is drinking, seems run down or maybe depressed, and has "blackouts," forgetting what he or she did, it's time for you to talk to your friend. If that doesn't work, go to the R.A. Your friend really needs help.

Drugs—Casual or Otherwise

In high school, doing drugs is considered cool. Here, it's really underground and you have to look for it if you want any drugs. Sometimes, when I find out who's doing drugs, I'm surprised.

Christina Hoffman, junior, Harvard University, Cambridge, MA

If you walk into a room and see a bag of mushrooms on the table, remember that no one likes the person who's going to the R.A. If people ask if you want to join them, just say, "Oh, I think I'll pass."

Paul Bromen, junior, St. Olaf, College, Northfield, MN

DID WE MENTION THAT . . .

One student talked about a roommate who was a self-declared stoner. Our student was uncomfortable having marijuana in the room, so the roommate would go out, smoke, and come back smelling of marijuana. One day, the university police knocked on the door while the roommate was playing Halo and our student was doing homework. He said, "My whole life flashed before my eyes. I thought I was going to lose everything I'd worked for." He left so officers could talk with the roommate, and when he returned, the officer was holding up a two-foot bong that our student had never seen before. The roommate is not at the university anymore.

I'd heard a lot of crazy things happen in college, but the shocker for me was that cocaine was just right there, at parties. I know what goes on, but to watch somebody snort a line in front of you is surprising.

Will Burton, junior, University of Oregon, Eugene

Freshman year was not that big a deal [regarding drugs] because I lived on a nonsmoking floor. Weed is the biggest drug because it's cheap. If people are allowed to smoke cigarettes, they think it also allows for weed. But it's not everywhere.

Greg Vanker, senior, Michigan State University, East Lansing

The largest drug problems here are using Ritalin and Ecstasy to study. The pressure is academic, not social.

Sandra Lazo de la Vega, sophomore, Florida Atlantic University, Wilkes Honors College, Jupiter

Most of what I know about drugs I learned when I came to college—and I've never even done them. Nothing good comes out of it. Selling/buying can get you into *big* trouble.

Amie Reed, junior, Illinois State University, Normal

Here, there's only a few people who aren't into the whole drinking thing, but some people drink a lot less and do it just socially. It's easy to find them.

James Balkam, freshman, West Virginia University, Morgantown

The best way to stay out of trouble is to find a good group of friends so you can have people you are comfortable with. If you are kind of floating socially, you might end up with people doing things you aren't comfortable with.

Ian Young, sophomore, Grinnell (IA) College

DID WE MENTION THAT . . .

If you feel pressure to do drugs or drink,
- it's time to run around with different people;
- you don't have to spend Friday nights at the library (options—dinner out, shopping, movies, city walks);
- figure you and your lifestyle are just fine.

Don't Drink? Don't Do Drugs?
Where to Find Friends Like You

I decided to wait until I was 21 to drink. It's a little rough, because everyone asks over and over if you want a drink. I think they ask because they don't feel they can have fun without alcohol. I knew I didn't need it. Party is pretty much part of me.

Annon Woodin, senior, Iowa State University, Ames

One of my big fears was that everyone would be partying, drinking, and staying up late and I'd be sitting alone in the dorm on Friday and Saturday nights. But it's a lot tamer than I had anticipated. All of a sudden I see other people also there, and we hang out. Maybe I found the right group of people who also aren't into partying.

Zack Barr, freshman, Brandeis University, Waltham, MA

I am glad I chose not to do drugs. I have seen alcoholism and drugs hurt people, and I have been hurt by others' lifestyles. It's hard to watch someone start at the top and slide to the bottom and then try to work back up the ladder. It is not an easy climb.

Alissa Busha, senior, University of Central Oklahoma, Oklahoma City

Do what you want to do and don't feel obligated.

Beth Giudicessi, senior, University of Notre Dame (IN)

Partying is mostly easy to tolerate as long as your roommate gives you warning that it will happen. If your roommate has a party in your room, you can go crash at a friend's or something. If you don't want to be around drugs and alcohol, just accept the fact that your roommate does and let that person do his or her thing.

Brittany Borstad, junior, Iowa State University, Ames

I really didn't go out to parties, so there was never an opportunity for peer pressure.

Tyler Sloss, sophomore, Duke University, Durham, NC

At every party you will find at least one other person who doesn't drink. I know people who won't drink and others who drink moderately.

Katy Cortese, freshman, University of Kansas, Lawrence

GET THIS! PEER PRESSURE— FOR SURE

Peer pressure can definitely buy into this because kids want to fit in, be cool, be social.

Cassius Harris, sophomore, Oberlin (OH) College

The pressure is implicit. People ask what you did last night or where you went. If you didn't go out, you're embarrassed to answer.

Emily Gravett, senior, Colgate University, Hamilton, NY

In college, people think you are judging them if you don't drink. They're apprehensive if you are just hanging out.

Paul Bromen, junior, St. Olaf College, Northfield, MN

GET THIS! PEER PRESSURE— NOT REALLY

Nobody cared if I didn't drink. That's cool. It's cold in the Midwest in the winter, and walking around to go to parties is not so fun. Peer pressure is not hard to avoid.

Greg Vanker, senior, Michigan State University, East Lansing

There's always marijuana about, but it was the same in high school, so it's not a big deal for anyone. People I know who have done drugs have not tried to talk me into it.

Maria Henning, junior, University of California–Berkeley

I went into college completely straight-edge and managed to go the entire first semester without drinking. That changed second semester, although I wouldn't call it peer pressure. I was just surprised at how lax everyone's attitude toward alcohol seemed to be. Still, I was careful, having my first drinks with my best friends.

David Neumann, sophomore, University of Southern California, Los Angeles

I don't go to parties with alcohol, but if we are in a room and friends have wine, that's okay.

Rachel Lenz, junior, Vassar College, Poughkeepsie, NY

I lived in a substance-free dorm with people who knew how to enjoy themselves without having to be under the influence of drugs or alcohol. It was by no means the stereotypical "geeky" group who stayed in on Friday night to study, but rather students who had interests other than just being "wasted." You can go out, enjoy yourself, have a few drinks, and come home to a place that doesn't reek of alcohol.

Sarah Fryc, senior, Colgate University, Hamilton, NY

If you don't drink, at first people are fine with it. But later, they start to pressure you. They just want to get you hooked once. It's funny for them to see you drunk, but you don't realize everybody is laughing at you. If you end up getting drunk, you won't even enjoy it.

Shakira Ali, sophomore, Loyola University, Chicago

While I've felt little alcohol or drug pressures, I felt a decent amount of pressure to "hook up" with people after/during parties. That's what you're supposed to do when you're drunk, right? While you may feel unattractive or uncool because you go home from a party by yourself, it's a lot better than realizing that you messed around with someone you don't care about, or even worse, with someone you do care about only to find out they only liked you when they were drunk.

Alix Lifka-Reselman, freshman, Brandeis University, Waltham, MA

Hey, Lend Me $20

Here's the truth: College costs suck the cash right out of your wallet before you've even counted the bills. Textbooks alone can cost as much as an airline ticket. Plus, there are lots of hidden costs—lattes, deodorant, and even bailing a friend out of jail. You'll need to set up a budget and—even harder—stick to it to avoid disasters such as spending $3,000 and you don't know where. Credit cards can ruin that budget—plastic is much easier than following your weekly budget. But there are ways to triumph: finding cheaper books, cheaper meals, and cheaper fun.

Where Did All That Money Go?

I never met anyone in college who has not asked that question verbatim.

Leor Benyamini, junior, Quinnipiac University, Hamden, CT

You can't just go to Wal-Mart and buy $100 worth of junk.

Nick Davidson, senior, Oklahoma State University, Stillwater

Before I left for college, I was making $600 a week. At school, I was making only a third of that, but still spending like I had all $600. You don't really realize this is happening at first if you're used to having plenty of spending money.

Jeff Eskew, senior, Texas Christian University, Fort Worth

If I ask my parents for money, they may think I'm being irresponsible. Actually, they underestimate the cost of being a college student. They'll assume I'm out drinking and partying, which I don't have time for.

Jade Hidle, senior, California State University, Long Beach

I have friends who spend $200 a week on alcohol for them and their roommates. And they're still in school. That's the weird thing.

Brian Steimers, junior, University of Delaware, Newark

> Don't loan money to a friend when you're drunk.
>
> *John Schmidt, senior, University of Kansas, Lawrence*

DID WE MENTION THAT . . .

Online poker in dorm rooms and on laptops in the back of lecture classes is as common as midnight pizza binges but with potentially worse consequences than gaining the Freshman 15. Besides addiction issues, you can pile up a mountain of debt that "one more hand" likely won't fix. Students have dropped out of school and one student even robbed a bank. That's more than a run of bad luck.

I met a bit of conflict when we got sick of the dorm food and were ordering or going out. However, I felt much better after I made over $1,000 playing online poker. I realize this is not a permanent solution and it has high risks, so I don't recommend it!

David Neumann, sophomore, University of Southern California, Los Angeles

Somehow I managed to go through almost $3,000 during the summer before and my first year of college, and I cannot honestly tell you what I spent it on.

Amie Reed, junior, Illinois State University, Normal

The money I received as graduation gifts was supposed to last me through my sophomore year. I think I ran out of cash around February of my freshman year.

Allison McAndrew, sophomore, Williams College, Williamstown, MA

Online shopping is so easy—and distracting. I go online when I'm bored. Say you've always wanted this one CD, and now it's within a couple of clicks.

Joe Kempf, senior, St. Olaf College, Northfield, MN

20/20 HINDSIGHT

You don't realize money problems are coming. At home with the safety net of parent money, you were just used to buying clothes and movie tickets, and now you have to re-budget for necessities like laundry, rent, and food.

Cristina Baptista, graduate student, Fordham University, Bronx, NY

Food, Glorious Food

My first grocery bill was 45 bucks. I was like, "*What?*" I had like seven things. Next time, I got stuff like generic peanut butter instead of Jiffy and the bill dropped to $15.

Brittany Borstad, junior, Iowa State University, Ames

You can get good foods like stir-fry and salad bars at school. But everything is weighed, so a few carrot sticks add up, and one day you don't have any points left on your card.

Jason Chen, junior, Vassar College, Poughkeepsie, NY

There can be some pressures to spend more than you may be comfortable with here, partially because the area around the school is quite affluent. I went to dinner a few times and was very conscious about what I got to eat because it was pricey.

Andrew Balkam, senior, Georgetown University, Washington, DC

I go to the grocery store more and talk my roommate into cooking or having dinner with me. It's no fun having to eat by myself.

Maria Henning, junior, University of California–Berkeley

Budget Smarts

When you first get to campus, figure out a budget that still allows you to have fun. Say, "I'll spend X dollars a month to have some fun and go out to eat once in awhile."

James Langlois, junior, Tulane University, New Orleans

I had worked at restaurants ever since I was 16, so I knew how much I made on average. I took that average and made out monthly budgets. If I worked a weekend, that would pay for rent. The rest would cover gas and food, plus you eat for a discount at the restaurant.

Lindsey Connolly, junior, Arizona State University, Tempe

Withdraw all the money you'll need for the month at the beginning of each month. Put it in a secret place and allot a certain amount to spend every week.

Akwasi Agyemang, sophomore, Boston University

I'm living on scholarships and grants and getting little from my parents. Except if I'm in a real jam, I'm on my own. If you know you are bad at spending and you get all your financial aid money at once, set up a monthly budget or it will be gone.

Aimee Ludlow, sophomore, Florida State University, Tallahassee

---

GET THIS! SUBSIDIZING ROOMMATES

Don't let your roommate borrow money or your car. I was going to meet my roommate at a party later. As I was walking out, I put cab money for her on the desk. Then, I said, "Oh, my God. I am not her dad." I picked up my money and left.

Rebecca Zwisler, senior, St. Mary's College, Notre Dame, IN

Some people buy a meal plan for the year and it's used up first semester. They're buying food for all their friends or getting the most expensive meal or just buying too much food.

Jennifer Bowen, sophomore, Westminster College, Salt Lake City

My summer work and job money was direct-deposited to my home bank account, and there was no debit or credit card available. That gave me enough for books and going out, with the rest contributing to tuition and room and board that scholarships did not cover. I'm not from a spendy culture.

Sarah Sentz, sophomore, University of Montana, Missoula

Balance your checkbook. I'll say it again. Balance your checkbook. It's a very bad idea not to know how much money is in your account.

Adam Berry, senior, Emory University, Atlanta

Textbook$

I had no idea how much books would cost. I got books for five core freshman classes. Each class had textbooks and other books costing about $150. I paid so much I will hold on to them my whole life.

Leor Benyamini, junior, Quinnipiac University, Hamden, CT

In high school, you paid $200 for textbooks for the entire year. Here, I pay $200 a quarter.

Elizabeth Joyce, sophomore, Stanford (CA) University

DID WE MENTION THAT . . .

If you sell your books back to the bookstore later on, they'll be worth a pittance of the original price. You think you'll be getting all this money back, but you won't.

When you sign up for a class, you receive the title and ISBN number for each book required. Type the numbers into a Web site like Amazon.com or half.com—a subsidiary of eBay. That will bring up all the books matching your ISBN numbers. I got a $130 math book for $8 because it was used. The corners were dented and the cover was scratched and some numbers were circled in pencil, but nothing that would deem it anywhere close to not using.

Will Burton, junior, University of Oregon, Eugene

GET THIS! WAIT TO BUY TEXTBOOKS ...

- until class meets three times and the professor says what he or she thinks of the required books. "Required" doesn't always mean required.
- if you already learned a lot of the material in high school thanks to a sharp teacher or AP class.
- until you know if the material will be on the tests. Sometimes, professors require two textbooks: one you'll be tested on and the other for background. If you go to class and take good notes, you might not need the background books.
- if you and a friend can take the same classes different semesters and trade books.
- if there's a reserved copy or two in the library—unless lots of other students have the same idea.

Not getting the books at all is another solution, though risky.

Andrew Balkam, senior, Georgetown University, Washington, DC

Find a way to pay for those books, even if you go broke doing it. You're not in college to do substandard work, and you're up against a lot of competition.

Jesse Herwitz, junior, Fordham University, New York

GET THIS! HOW USED IS THAT USED BOOK?

- Is the book held together by a thread (literally)?
- Are pages missing? Stuck together with ... yuck!?
- Has every sentence been highlighted? Do highlighted words look like a yellow measles epidemic on the pages?
- Are margin notes correct, misleading, or written over the text? Mindless doodles are fine, especially on slow days.
- Is it the correct edition?

Keep the books in your major. They will pay for themselves in the long run. Get rid of the rest.

Meghan Hannahs, junior, Westminster College, Salt Lake City

During the first couple of weeks of school, the bookstore gives out goodie bags with CDs, shampoo, razors and book bags—plus 10 percent off T-shirts and things for your parents. They always want stickers for their cars.

Cristina Baptista, graduate student, Fordham University, Bronx, NY

Living on Plastic

My parents gave me a credit card for emergencies. I thought an emergency was whenever I wanted something. Then the bill came and they said, "How could you spend that much at Wal-Mart?"

Rebecca Zwisler, senior, St. Mary's College, Notre Dame, IN

I never thought my debit card gave me the ability to spend as much as I wanted because the money I put on it was the same money I took out.

Will Burton, junior, University of Oregon, Eugene

I put a lot of cash on my college debit card in case I needed it. I spent more because it was there. I used it on impulsive snack-type items such as at the bakery across the street.

Jason Chen, junior, Vassar College, Poughkeepsie, NY

GET THIS! NEED VS. WANT REALITY CHECK

▶ Financially strapped student: "Hey, I *need* money for my daily Starbucks fix.

Reality: "Hey, you *want* money for Starbucks. You *need* money for a box of Tide."

You'll get 20 or 30 letters a semester from companies offering you their credit card, but have your parents help you get one. I have a $500 limit on mine, and it's helping me build up good credit.

Brittany Borstad, junior, Iowa State University, Ames

DID WE MENTION THAT . . .

▶ Credit card companies often give away free swag on campus to entice you to sign up for their card. Great in the moment, but not worth it in the long run. There is no such thing as "no strings attached."

Credit cards have a limit for a reason, so you shouldn't have two cards, each with a $500 limit.

Nick Davidson, senior, Oklahoma State University, Stillwater

BELIEVE IT! OUT OF MONEY, OUT OF THE APARTMENT, OUT OF SCHOOL

We heard about a student who signed up for two or three credit cards and charged everything. He'd say, "I'll get lunch today." Finally, his parents cut him off. He tried juggling his normal spending without access to his parents' deep pockets. But he couldn't keep up with the bills if he continued taking the same number of credit hours. So he took off a semester, moved out of the apartment he shared and into a free basement bedroom. Even that wasn't enough. It took him three years to get back on his feet.

Do *not* get a credit card right away. You might think it is easy to handle and you won't spend too much on it, but that is *not true*!! I have only had my credit card for three months and I have been paying thousands of dollars for it. It is *ridiculous*!!

Lauren Krpan, sophomore, University of Mississippi, Oxford

DID WE MENTION THAT . . .

Using your parents' credit card probably won't guarantee a free ride because

1. Parents look at what you charge each month.
2. If you charge a subscription to *Entertainment Weekly*, a plane ticket to Cancun, or your very own karaoke system, they will ask why.
3. "Because I need a break from school" will not fly as a response.
4. Actually, we can't think of any response that will fly.
5. Even worse, you'll have to pay them back. Maybe even soon.

GET THIS! CREDIT CARD DEBT RESCUE

You can dig out of your credit card debt without standing in soup lines, holding down three jobs, and dropping out of college. Suggestions:

- Seek advice from your school's financial aid officer.
- Don't have multiple credit cards. You only need one.
- Send your credit cards to your parents and go cash-only.
- Pay more than the minimum monthly balance.
- Ask your credit card company to give you a lower interest rate. It might work.
- Ask your parents to pay the bill and you pay them back to avoid hefty interest charges.
- Chart out what you've charged and mend some spendy ways.

Hit by Hidden Costs

Public transportation if you're going to school in a city.

James Langlois, junior, Tulane University, New Orleans

Cleaning supplies and lightbulbs for your room, a desk lamp, and batteries.

Katie Loberg, junior, Loyola University, Chicago

Things you forgot at home: nail clippers, blank CDs, socks, a decent-sized trash can.

Mike Husni, junior, University of Delaware, Newark

My girlfriend. She's traditional and likes when I treat. We're always going out for something. For example, I had to pay for some supplies for her today because she didn't have money or her ATM card.

Greg Vanker, senior, Michigan State University, East Lansing

Filing for financial aid late.

Adam Berry, senior, Emory University, Atlanta

Car problems. Change the oil and spark plugs and this and this, and suddenly it's $300.

Aimee Ludlow, sophomore, Florida State University, Tallahassee

Library fines and dorm events like ski trips to Tahoe or camping trips or concerts.

Elizabeth Joyce, sophomore, Stanford (CA) University

Parking your car. It's $300 to $500 a semester on this campus. The campus police will wait five minutes by your car for the meter to be up so they can give you a ticket. My neighbor covered his whole wall with parking tickets by the end of the semester.

Brian Steimers, junior, University of Delaware, Newark

Cell phone bill. I'd say to my parents, "If you give me the money, what can I do to work it off?" I didn't like handouts from anybody.

John Schmidt, senior, University of Kansas, Lawrence

Bailing someone out of jail. I had to, and it can be costly, especially when you are required to wait a certain amount of time before repayment.

Amie Reed, junior, Illinois State University, Normal

GET THIS! PAYING JOBS = POCKET MONEY

- Sperm or blood donor
- Psych department research subject where for maybe $30, you keep track of how many cups of coffee you drink a week
- On-campus jobs: clerical, lifeguard, recreation building monitor, groundskeeper, intramural soccer referee
- Hotel night desk clerk because you're probably awake anyway
- Tutoring students at a nearby high school
- Babysitting for your professor—teachers like to go out once in awhile, too

GET THIS! FIVE FAST MONEY SAVERS

1. Skip feeding vending machines that gobble 85 cents for a package of 10 potato chips.
2. Buy your plane ticket for winter break in September, not November.
3. Swap clothes with friends.
4. Never pay full price for anything except your mom's birthday present.
5. Hide your sneakers every time the vision of a mall passes before you.

Thank goodness for my grandfather—he sends me an allowance to call him. My parents don't send me money. I still call them.

Laura Polden, freshman, George Washington University, Washington, DC

Really Cheap Fun

- Play croquet on the quad.

- Pick up seasonal fresh food at the farmers' market.

- Find unlimited, all-night bowling for 50 cents a game.

- Set up a Scrabble tournament.

- See if the library provides access to video cameras and state-of-the-art editing programs. Then put together something fun. Or better yet, something stupid.

- Patronize shops and restaurants that give student discounts.

- Use the campus wellness center facilities rather than off-campus private gyms.

- Know which bars have the cheapest drink specials and which clubs charge no cover on which nights.

- Go to a museum on free admission day or evening.

You can go to a lot of parties and, afterward, have no memory of having a great time or building a meaningful relationship. But it only cost about $5.

Kevin Spahn, senior, University of Minnesota–Minneapolis

Second Semester and Beyond

You've got friends; you've got your first-semester grades. Now you can figure out the other parts of school. Second semester is all about making choices that affect the rest of your college career. You need to find out who knows best about classes and professors and whether you must decide your major right now. Studying abroad junior or senior year takes planning, starting now. If you keep mulling over transfer options, some of our students share what pushed them to another school. Even decisions about spring break—go home, to the beach, or maybe even Budapest—make second semester race by way too fast.

Back on Campus

I was more open second semester. You've had a whole semester of experience and you get a fresh start at a new semester. For me, this was when I really started to enjoy being in college.
Amie Reed, junior, Illinois State University, Normal

Second semester is a little nerve-racking because you realize your group of friends has changed. First semester, people tend to be friends with their roommates, the people in their dorm, and whomever they happened to meet first. Second semester, you begin to find the people who are going to be your close friends, potentially for the rest of college.

Gina Turrini, junior, Amherst (MA) College

DID WE MENTION THAT . . .

> A critical mistake is thinking old friends back home have totally forgotten you, moved on, so you should, too. The reality is they probably miss you as much as you miss them so text-message or IM friends and meet up with them when you're home. Keep the connection.

I definitely didn't want break to end. But I didn't feel as weird as when I first moved here. And all my stuff is here.

Diane Hennan, freshman, Saint Ambrose University, Davenport, IA

GET THIS! BY NOW . . .

> - You know where to go for cheap eats, late-night grub, and a cup of coffee that's actually good.
> - When you say, "I'm going home," you mean to your dorm room.

I had gotten my grades and it was kind of like, "Okay, that was hard but you didn't fail; in fact, you did okay work." Then you can figure out what you need to do and have a better balance between play and study.

Beth Giudicessi, senior, University of Notre Dame (IN)

20/20 **HINDSIGHT**

First semester I had lofty goals. I was going to be a doctor. I took really intensive courses, and I realized that was not for me. Second semester I took classes in random courses and figured out what I was really interested in.

Jennifer Herlihy, senior, University of California–Berkeley

You have $3^1/2$ years left, so if you don't have all your ducks in a row the first semester, it'll be okay. If you have to drop a class or take a class over, it'll be okay.

Martha Edwards, senior, Marquette University, Milwaukee

Where to Get the Best Advice

Having a roommate from the area is definitely convenient.

Brian Steimers, junior, University of Delaware, Newark

A senior who is a friend of a friend of a friend, if you can get to that person.

Akwasi Agyemang, sophomore, Boston University

DID WE MENTION THAT . . .

> One nontraditional student we know says, "Understand that everything hinges on you." That can be really good or really bad, depending on the kind of day you're having.

Juniors and seniors know things about the campus, classes, professors, how to get things done because they've been through this.

Adam Berry, senior, Emory University, Atlanta

My adviser is good for the requirements. I turn to upperclass people I trust for advice such as, can I do 22 credits and which professors are good.

Katie Beno, freshman, Gonzaga University, Spokane, WA

GET THIS! WHY DIDN'T SOMEBODY TELL *ME* . . .

- Even within the requirements, there are so many variations that you can find a required class that interests you.
- You might be able to take an incomplete in a class and finish it later.
- Research grant money is out there if you just go looking.
- Just because somebody says there's a party at 2 A.M. does not mean you have to get up and go.

20/20 HINDSIGHT

There's a lot to be said for getting to know the people who educate you. Get to know someone who is passionate about a particular subject, even if you don't have other similar interests. You can only talk to Mom on the phone, so having another adult to ask, "Is this a good idea, or should I approach the situation another way?" is really helpful.

Kendra Boeckman, senior, Oklahoma State University, Stillwater

With advising, you are pretty much on your own, at least in my college (architecture). The advisers know less than you if you've gone online to find out information.

Maria Henning, junior, University of California–Berkeley

Choosing a Major . . . or Not

I don't know how you can be expected to know what you want to do with the rest of your life when you're 18 years old.

Amie Reed, junior, Illinois State University, Normal

A declared major is not set in stone. You always have a choice, even if it's your last semester in college.

Jade Hidle, senior, California State University–Long Beach

20/20 HINDSIGHT

I have been every Arts and Sciences major there is, from chemistry and biology to communications, and history, political science, a religion minor, sociology, psychology . . . yes, I don't know what area is left that I haven't touched on. I think I have one picked now. The worst is getting to your junior year and realizing that you have 92 hours of chemistry and your real passion is art history.

Adrienne May, sophomore, University of Missouri–Kansas City

Not knowing your major is a big cause of freshman stress. But you don't need to know until second semester sophomore year. Just take general classes until then.

Ande Davis, senior, Washburn University, Topeka, KS

I declared my major when I registered for classes as a freshman. You can know at that point. If you have a passion for something, don't be deterred from saying anything freshman year.

Scott Beggs, senior, Baylor University, Waco, TX

I really like psych courses, but took a Latin American politics course (senior level) first semester. I was in way over my head, but I built a good relationship with a professor, whom I met at orientation. Now, I'm pulled this way and that way.

Sandra Lazo de la Vega, sophomore, Florida Atlantic University, Wilkes Honors College, Jupiter

---

DID WE MENTION THAT . . .

It's so annoying when all your parents' friends ask, "What's your major?" It's even more annoying when your own parents decide they'll help you decide.

Start thinking from Day 1 what you want to do. I told the T.A. for my general freshman engineering class that I was interested in materials science engineering. Within two weeks she hooked me up with an MSE grad student and I started doing (unpaid) research with him and his professor. This experience and networking can give you a big leg up when it comes to applying for admission to the (specific) college and future resumes and recommendations.

Chris Petz, senior, University of Washington, Seattle

GET THIS! HOW INTERNSHIPS SOLIDIFY MAJORS

> I've taken off two semesters to work full-time, paid internships that had me doing more than just getting coffee for people. When I came back, I was taking classes on half the stuff I did on the internships. Memorizing material makes much more sense if you have seen and done it in the real world.
>
> *Greg Vanker, senior, Michigan State University, East Lansing*

I'm a management major, which I chose sophomore year. I haven't decided if it's a perfect fit. But I like it, and it provides a general knowledge base. With any job you get, you'll have to take additional training anyway.

Lauren Press, junior, University of Denver

You'll know if you should change majors. I wasn't interested in what my science professors were saying, made excuses not to go to class, avoided doing assignments and reading the text. I didn't care if I got an A or an F on a test. But I was becoming really focused on English and writing classes, and never missed them, even when I was sick.

Fadi Bayaa, junior, California State University–Long Beach

How-I-Found-My-Major Stories

Andrew Balkam, senior, Georgetown University, Washington, DC, found an old piano on the basement floor of his dorm, plunked out some tunes, and decided to go back after quitting lessons four years before. He's earning a music minor.

Jason Kaplan, senior, Colgate University, Hamilton, NY, was thinking he wanted to major in poli sci; his dad was thinking Jason wanted to go into law. No matter, he had to take Intro to Oceanography to fulfill a requirement. He really liked the professor, took more courses from him, and loved the labs. He ended up majoring in geology—and he's going to law school.

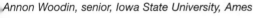

Human Sexuality class was required for my major. The first day of class with hundreds of people, our teacher says to get everybody comfortable, we should yell out slang terms for male and female anatomy—purple-headed warrior, one-man canoe, bone collector. I got bright red. I was way too innocent for this class. Another day, she decides we need to watch the video, "60 and Still Doing It." Everyone in the class is disgusted.
Annon Woodin, senior, Iowa State University, Ames

DID WE MENTION THAT . . .

▶ Unless you are comatose, you are painfully aware that parents worry about job security and health insurance.

Although *Lori Donovan, junior, St. Olaf College, Northfield, MN,* was going to be content with just a math major, she wondered if she could pull off an English major. She registered for one class, loved it, and is an English-math double major.

Mike Husni, junior, University of Delaware, Newark, considered a theater major, but his parents disapproved. He looked at engineering, but was not interested in what he thought he would be doing professionally. So he's pursuing a career that will make him happy, but not rich—education with an emphasis in drama.

It took *Greg Vanker, senior, Michigan State University, East Lansing,* five semesters and a lot of classes exploring options in engineering. Finally, he took a packaging class (almost everything you buy comes in a package). "I thought it was a joke major—little did I know. It's similar to engineering but not in the engineering college. I love it."

The first big test for *Katharine McCormick, sophomore, University of Pennsylvania, Philadelphia,* was in math. She'd done okay on the practice test. But one question was really geared toward engineering and with only six or seven questions, if you missed one, it wasn't good. She liked math, but not enough to take the next class. Now she's a comparative literature–Hispanic studies double major.

Lisa Moody, freshman, University of Nebraska, Omaha, job-shadowed the summer before college with a speech pathologist and found her major.

Christina Hoffman, junior, Harvard University, Cambridge, MA, expected relevant (freshman) courses about politics in her prospective government major. Instead, she ended up in pretty dry theoretical courses. So she declared as an English major. But as a sophomore, she realized she really wanted to work in politics. She switched back to the government major, figuring she could read the classics on her own.

GET THIS! TIME OFF TO FIND A MAJOR

Sarah Sentz, sophomore, University of Montana, Missoula, e-mailed, "I wasn't sure what I wanted to major in, I was getting burned out, and it was silly (and expensive!) to continue with no direction. After I decided to take the year off, I realized I want to go into nursing. I applied to a volunteer organization and am headed to Ghana for six months to probably work in a health care setting. This will give me amazing practical experience and also the opportunity to travel and experience Ghanian culture. I'm excited with my decision even though it means practically starting over to fulfill the requirements."

Spring Break—Utopia or Myth?

A lot of teenagers think they are completely invincible and nothing bad will happen to them. But bad things can happen on spring break.

Rebecca Zwisler, senior, St. Mary's College, Notre Dame, IN

I am on spring break right now on South Padre Island and it is ridiculous.

E-mail message from Paul Bromen, junior, St. Olaf College, Northfield, MN

GET THIS! SUNSHINE MISSIONS

> More students are getting beach time as they don hard hats to help others in warm spots. From placement through not-for-profit organizations, students help clean up areas from natural disasters or rebuild houses, among other chores. Maybe *that's* a spring break the parents would be glad to fund.

Spring break in Cancun or Miami is a big myth for a lot of students. You don't have money and your parents don't have money after paying for your college. The majority go home. The most depressing thing would be to sit in the dorm when everybody else is gone.

Shakira Ali, sophomore, Loyola University, Chicago

Spring break is all about hooking up. If you want to be into that, go where there's a crazy atmosphere.

Joanna Stone, senior, University of Mississippi, Oxford

As a good professor friend of mine put it—no bugs, no babies, no broken hearts. Follow the 3B's and you're good.

Luke Roth, freshman, Loyola University, Chicago

Spring break is stereotypical. Always warm, always way too much skin showing.

Katie Jozwik, junior, Columbia College, Chicago

If your spring break isn't at the same time as your friends' breaks on other campuses, visit them, see their school, and meet their new friends.

Christine Fletcher, junior, Bates College, Lewiston, ME

GET THIS! NO, THANKS, TO HEADING HOME

I was once advised never to go home for spring break. At first I didn't understand this logic, but when I went to Jamaica, I understood. Spring break is supposed be about letting go of all the stress that has built up that year. Chances are that going home and sitting on your ass all day won't have the same stress release as going to distant lands with your friends.

Aaron Castro, junior, United States Naval Academy, Annapolis, MD

I went to Cancun with my family. Everyone at school was getting sick, lots of papers to do, and then into a bathing suit and warm weather—that got me through the last weeks of school.

Zack Barr, freshman, Brandeis University, Waltham, MA

This was my last spring break at home. At Thanksgiving it's exciting, and everyone says, "Oh, I missed you." Then I came home for semester break and my sister had taken over my room. And spring break is just a week in the middle of the semester and I have work to do.

Laura Polden, freshman, George Washington University, Washington, DC

Freshman spring break was a disaster! I was supposed to go to a conference in Philly (Philadelphia) for which I had received a grant. Instead, I fell under the axe of Providence weather and ended up with pneumonia. However, my boyfriend was amazing and took care of me during the entire time.

Sri Kalyanaraman, junior, Brown University, Providence, RI

GET THIS! SPRING BREAK IN . . . BUDAPEST?

Twelve of us rented an apartment in Budapest—$110 each for the week and we all used our money, not our parents'. It was very, very cold. We walked everywhere or took the subway. Eight people went to Vienna one day. You could go into every church where you heard organ music. There were a lot of friendly people. I was taken for a Hungarian guide a couple of times. I learned how to count to 11, say "Yes" and "No," and, eventually, "Thank you."

Katharine McCormick, sophomore, University of Pennsylvania, Philadelphia

Professors have an unspoken agreement to assign papers due or give exams the day you come back from spring break. That makes it difficult to go for a drunken week in Mexico.

Jade Hidle, senior, California State University–Long Beach

Studying Abroad

Some people are afraid of missing something if they go abroad. Whatever's happening at school can't compare with what's going on in the program. You won't have an experience like that for the rest of your life.

Christine Fletcher, junior, Bates College, Lewiston, ME

Two friends who were juniors studied at the place in Japan where I am going now. We e-mailed a lot about what each of them saw and was doing. By the time I applied my sophomore year, I knew four people who had done that program and the classes they took.

Rachel Lenz, junior, Vassar College, Poughkeepsie, NY

One of the appeals of the program is not knowing people because it will make me more independent. The experience will re-center me and help me figure out what I'm going to do with my life.

Jennifer Herlihy, senior, University of California–Berkeley

DID WE MENTION THAT . . .

Going on a study-abroad program with your friends is like rooming with your best friend when you get to college—unless you split up to meet and do things with other people.

Everything about a country that is fun and cool and different starts to get annoying after three months because the novelty wears off. You'll want to go back to America where there's Wal-Mart and stores are open late.

Henna Messina, senior, Fordham University, New York

Choose a program where you are not surrounded by all American students but still everyone speaks English–it makes life easier. I now have friends from Germany, Spain, England, Italy, Japan, and Poland.

Molly Egan, fourth year of five-year program, University of Tennessee, Knoxville, e-mailing from Krakow, Poland

I didn't go because my college wasn't affiliated with the program I'd chosen, so there would be a problem transferring credits. Also, it's expensive. You can't get a Pell Grant to study abroad.

Shakira Ali, sophomore, Loyola University, Chicago

GET THIS! DO THIS NOW TO STUDY ABROAD LATER

- Go to an informational program, if for no other reason than to see what's possible.
- Plan your academic schedule early so you'll graduate on time.
- Figure out the room situation if you'll be gone only one semester.
- Get a written guarantee that the units you earn will transfer and apply to your major.
- Pick a location where you'll get better at a foreign language you're already studying.

BELIEVE IT! STUDENT GETS RABIES SHOTS AFTER DOG ATTACK

One late night as two American students on holiday in Budapest were heading down dark stairs to a bar, two German shepherds attacked the first student. One dog bit her arm while the other latched onto her leg "for what seemed like a minute." The students screamed and someone finally called off the dogs, assuring the young women the dogs were healthy. There was "lots of blood," a trip to the hospital, and the student refusing the first needle the doctor brought for a tetanus shot because the needle was not in a sterile package.

When they returned to their Austrian university, the bites were infected. The foreign student adviser said the student must get rabies shots immediately because the dogs could not be positively identified now. She called her dad in the United States to ask if she really needed the shots. He said, "Well, the downside is if the dog does have rabies and you get it, you'll die." She got the shots.

"It didn't stop me from continuing to travel because bad things can happen no matter where you go. I guess the only lesson is to stick up for yourself, like make sure you don't get someone else's needle stuck in you. Everything else about the semester was fantastic."

GET THIS! STREET SMARTS FOR EVERYWHERE ABROAD

- Go somewhere so safe your parents will hardly worry.
- Alcohol and secondhand smoke are everywhere in Europe.
- Leave detailed information about where you'll be with family members.
- Drop the baseball cap, buy a jacket at a secondhand store, and don't advertise that you're an American.
- See our section on Personal Safety in Chapter 6. Those suggestions are good for pretty much every country.

The biggest adjustment was not being in Europe but being alone in a big city [London]. I lived in a flat, not knowing where I was, figuring out my way around. That summer taught me I need to stay in a small city, but I know what it's like to live in a glamorous city.

Beth Giudicessi, senior, University of Notre Dame (IN)

Should You Transfer?

It took me until the end of second trimester to truly get a feel for the college. I had considered transferring multiple times, but in the end, I realized I was not giving myself time to adjust. My mind wasn't always open to everything Mercyhurst had to offer.

Jackie Kohler, sophomore, Mercyhurst College, Erie, PA

My mom's answer to everything Chicago–the cold, the wind–is to transfer back to Texas.

Shakira Ali, sophomore, Loyola University, Chicago

I transferred (from a midwestern college) to the University of Montana because I was homesick for the land.

Sarah Sentz, sophomore, University of Montana, Missoula

If your school doesn't fit at first, I'd recommend not giving up. Instead, find new ways to look for your niche before starting from scratch at another school.

Katie Ablan, sophomore, Indiana University–Bloomington

> It's okay to realize this environment is not for you and to go somewhere else.
>
> *Erin Pirruccello, sophomore, University of Pennsylvania, Wharton School, Philadelphia*

GET THIS! A TWO-TIME TRANSFER SPECIALIST

A student who transferred twice largely for financial reasons (from extremely expensive even with scholarship money, to moderately expensive, to inexpensive) tells us that it's healthy and exciting to try out a new place (the extremely expensive school) as a young adult. But you shouldn't feel obligated to stay if it's making life miserable and stressful. If you do transfer, realize you're probably not going to have the "typical" college experience. But the upside is you'll learn to become independent, enterprising, and grateful.

GET THIS! SEAN'S TOUGH DECISION

I wasn't unhappy at Vanderbilt and dreaded the thought of having to make new friends and learning the intricacies and quirks of a new place. I realized, however, that I had only four years to get everything I wanted out of my undergraduate education and Harvard offered what I wanted. I also knew I could keep in close contact with people in Nashville. It was a tough decision, but one I am glad I made. Don't be timid. You can never get your college years back.

Sean Harris, junior, Harvard University, Cambridge, MA

I figured I was in the wrong place because I talked to my mom too much on the phone, didn't have any friends, went home almost every weekend, and had no idea what I was doing with my life. When I decided to transfer to NYU, I actually had a major I wanted to go into and more opportunities to do stuff in NYC. I felt a bit hesitant—for about a second.

Robyn Lee, junior, New York University, New York

I felt lots of pressure from different people who knew I had always wanted to go to college in Seattle and were concerned I was transferring here because of my boyfriend. They just wanted to make me sure of my choice. Once I made all the decisions, it's worth it.

Melissa Triber, sophomore, Central Washington University, Ellensburg, WA

Transferring was scary because I was really starting over socially and it was lonely. I wasn't living in a dorm and meeting people through freshman-oriented groups. My friends were mostly other transfer students I met by chance and initiative. Nobody holds your hand, and other people may already have a social group from freshman year. This is not to say that most people will not be open to having new friends; it's just that you will be conscious of the fact that they already have some.

Megan Marsh, graduate student, University of North Carolina at Chapel Hill

My high school sent the wrong transcripts, so I ended up at a school other than where I wanted to go. I knew within four weeks I would transfer. I had arrived at my first college with 21 college credits, but when I told somebody at orientation I'd already had some of the classes, they didn't know what to tell me. I wasn't making friends, which had never happened before. I wondered if I was homesick, but that really wasn't the case. I had friends at TCU, so I transferred.

Jeff Eskew, senior, Texas Christian University, Fort Worth

DID WE MENTION THAT . . .

One student simplified second semester to this: All you need to do right now is stay in school, make it to the next year. Every decision you make freshman year can be undone. Okay, almost every decision. Letting your life get completely out of control isn't easy to bounce back from.

Epilogue

So now you're a pro at figuring out this college thing, from making friends to surviving three mega research papers due the same week to partying. Agreed, college can be overwhelming, underwhelming, scary, exciting—sometimes all on the same day. Still, you can survive your mistakes and relish your successes. We found two threads woven through our students' conversations and e-mails. First, you change, your parents change, and you all grow just a little bit more in different ways. Second, you may not immediately take the bright shining path, but you can learn from your missteps and be successful. This book has been students speaking with you. Appropriately, they should have the last words.

Did Your Parents Get Smarter Since You Left Home?

They've always been smart. They're amazing!

Sri Kalyanaraman, junior, Brown University, Providence, RI

This comes more from learning to live on your own and not having your parents do everything for you. Now you're filing taxes, making doctor's appointments, paying bills on time. You say, "Oh, my parents actually do know what they are talking about. When did that happen?"

Adam Berry, senior, Emory University, Atlanta

I just learned to appreciate them more if I don't have to live under their roof.

Maria Henning, junior, University of California–Berkeley

Our relationship changed. When I went home after a few months at school, I realized what goes on at home and what makes things work. It was easier to notice stresses at home like pressure in the workplace and how hard my parents have tried to raise us. My parents seem a lot more human than they used to be.

Jason Chen, junior, Vassar College, Poughkeepsie, NY

Even though they are your parents, you can remind them you are now an independent person and you may not always take the path they wanted you to take.

Niki Grangruth, senior, St. Olaf College, Northfield, MN

> I talk to my parents about things I didn't used to. There's no sensor in my head anymore about what to say when I talk to them.
>
> *Beth Giudicessi, senior, University of Notre Dame (IN)*

Once I was in college, my dad started telling me his own college stories.

Brian Steimers, junior, University of Delaware, Newark

Final Thoughts

The toughest lesson (freshman year) is learning to be responsible for yourself when your parents aren't there to pick you up when you fall down.

Austin Hudson, freshman, Mississippi State University, Starkville

If your freshman grades are bad, you'll spend the rest of your time at college trying to make them better.

Dan Isaacs, junior, State University of New York–Binghamton

I definitely wish that I'd have made a stronger attempt to join more clubs and meet more people rather than hanging out solely with the people I lived with first semester.

Allison McAndrew, sophomore, Williams College, Williamstown, MA

During my freshman year, my dad was sick (back home in New York). I had a deep reliance on Tufts friends because they were the only ones here. They became my go-to, my support system. That sculpted my freshman year. If it had been a normal year, I might have been more critical, fickle, picky.

Katia Porzecanski, sophomore, Tufts University, Medford, MA

Be grateful for the opportunity to further your education. There are people not only in the United States who wish they could have what you have, but people throughout the world who would die to be where you are. And it is never too early to begin to prepare for the day you graduate.

Eric Jaron Mallet, junior, Abilene (TX) Christian University, e-mailing from Montevideo, Uruguay

Before you leave for school, make peace with the city you are living in (unless you're staying there for college). That city will cease to be "home" after Christmas break—your college city will become home. Even if you return after you get done with school, the town in which you grew up will never be the same.

Luke Roth, freshman, Loyola University, Chicago

Freshman year goes way too fast—it's over before you know it.

Colleen Johnson, freshman, Webster University, St. Louis, MO

Resources

Parents

College Parents of America—Nonprofit organization that advocates for services for college students. www.collegeparents.org

LDOnline—Guide to learning disabilities for parents, children, and teachers. www.ldonline.com

Books

Don't Tell Me What to Do, Just Send Money: The Essential Guide to the College Years, Helen E. Johnson and Christine Schelhas-Miller

Letting Go: A Parent's Guide to Understanding the College Years, Karen Levin Coburn and Madge Lawrence Treeger

Health

National Eating Disorders Association. www.edap.org

National Institutes of Health's National Institute on Drug Abuse—Support groups can be found through local public health agencies. http://www.nida.nih.gov/

Alcoholics Anonymous. www.alcoholics-anonymous.org

Money

Compare credit card rates, annual fees, and more at sites www.CardWeb.com and www.bankrate.com

Academic Financial Solutions. www.academicfinancial.com